One Spark

"Imagination Begins with You…" 2019

Various Authors

One Spark
"Imagination Begins with You…" 2019

Compiled by Brian Claspell

Library of Congress Control Number: 2019941877

Cover design by Jasmine Mumford

Interior design by Jasmine Mumford and Brian Claspell

ISBN: 978-1-947315-02-0

ACKNOWLEDGMENTS

Many people have helped judge and make this high school writing contest possible. The stories are great.

I LOVE IT!

Thanks to all of the judges. Thanks to all of the teachers and administrators who encourage their students to participate. Thanks to all of the students who send in the stories. Thanks to my family who let me take a few weekends to judge. Thanks to my wife who prepares the awards and supports me in so many other ways.

2019 Winners and Finalists

Winner: True Colors   by Jorja Grace Heinkel

Second Place: I'm Sorry   by Crista Ramsey

Honorable Mentions:

A Dance to Remember	by JaKayla Cornish
No Colors in the Middle East	by Amineh Ayyad
JACK	by Alexander Flint
Blue	by Georgia Ringstaff
Nobody Stays	by Kimberly Lau
Trouble In Paradise	by Grace Silva
Father's Promise	by James Sam

Finalists:

Story	Author	Story	Author
Interview with Emanuel Quena	Jada Broome	Wobbly	Iris Wright
Until the Last Time	Autumn Hakes	How You See Me	Jazzmyne Robinson
After life	Ashna Vithal Divekar	Why I'm The Way I Am	Peter Pham
The Enlightenment	Chloe Cattaneo	Peanut Butter Cups	Jessie Zheng
For the Love of Suzanna	Kaitlyn Gorman	The Mess	Kathryn Howard
A Stop in Time	Michael Kelly	North, South, East, and Ferdinand	Lady Ironmill
To Have a Purpose	Diana Farhat	A Rainy Day	Megan Lovejoy
Panic Attack	Elexus A Lopez	Xenon's Unending Turbulence: The Beginning	Alexandra Clark
Granuaile the Tumblr Queen	Autumn Hill	Dog Days	Mickilina Volpi
Flying Solo	Leah Thorley	Magic Trick	Ivy Moore
A Redeeming Finale	Julianna Feit	A Self-edited Comic	Kyndal Bree Harrison
My own Life	Jose Alfredo	Deja Vu	Nicholas Emington
The Day It All Changed	Virginia Hughes	Theo	Omid Mogasemi
Winter Is A Wonderland	Paige Weinstein	Grass	Anna
Ambedo	Queenie Quan	Late Night Contact Shenanigan	Evelyn Woo
Forever Young	Ashlyn Athey	The End of the Rainbow	Willow Scott
The Strange	Miracle N Etuakwu	The Observer	Laura Calzada
Mystery	Mia Carrillo	The Pen is Mightier than the Sword	Pranay Sharma
Weapon N-074	Lia Ahmed-Zaid	Resurgam	Victoria Shanks
A Familiar Face	Acsa Hemandez		

CONTENTS

SECTION 1 - YESTERDAY

No Colors in the Middle East

By Amineh Ayyad (Finalist and Honorable Mention)

Bang, pop, crackle! A myriad of sparks dance across the sky in what looks both synchronized and abstract. The world becomes a slide of film, repeatedly transcending into darkness only to be flashed back into reality through streaks of color. The warm shades of purple contrast neon greens, and the people of the town – spots among the sea of light– stare in awe at the firework display before them. As a child, I couldn't help but wonder how the fireworks fled the sky. Did they turn into dust, reverting into powdered forms? Or did they never leave, simply blending into the sky's velvet exterior? I concluded that the best explanation was this: the fireworks must have melted. I knew from experience that keeping colorful crayons outside created a puddle of color, and fireworks are nothing more than colors of the sky, so they must drip onto the ground! I wished I could find a place where the sky kissed the earth. I imagined the beauty of bright blue clouds touching the smooth greens of grass.

My imagination transcended me away from the crowd

and towards the trees for a better view. I followed the path into the brush, not thinking of the people behind me, and most definitely not considering who could appear before me. As I stumbled onto a sidewalk - scuffing my bright-pink sneakers – I saw kids that looked like me but weren't quite the same. These kids had thin clothes, long heads of hair, and no shoes – which was not fit for playing outside. I concluded that these kids must be looking for melted fireworks, too!

I ran up to the children with looks of confusion crossing their faces. "Do you guys need help? I'm great at finding things!" The tallest child, a dark boy with a skinny frame, stepped forward. "You shouldn't be here," he said with a scowl on his face. I always knew making friends could be hard, so I persisted to be nice. "I would love to play! I'm searching for something right now." A small girl squirmed her way to the front of the group. "What are you looking for?" she asked. Not entirely sure, I simply told her "Puddles of color." The other kids, clearly intrigued, looked at each other and then to the first boy, as if waiting for approval. "Well," he started, "we shouldn't be out for too long, so let's go." I initially didn't understand his concern; kids are always out playing!

Our group hiked through streets with rubble I have never noticed before, glancing at the sky for signs of color. I'm not sure if these kids have ever seen fireworks before; they looked a lot more scared than they should have been. I couldn't wait to see the looks on their faces when they finally saw the splashes of color! As the journey continued, I began to grow tired; however the other children, despite their tired appearances, seemed filled with energy. They marched on as if they had been trained for walks much longer than this one, showing no signs of hunger or fatigue. I wondered why I never saw these kids before. There are plenty of kids like them in my school and neighborhood, but something about them was... foreign. It was as if they were acting a role I have never watched on TV nor read in any book. The houses we passed cried with distress, tarps covering the holes where doors should be and roof should lay. The deeper we traveled into the town, the more lost I felt. This feeling – like I was walking into uncharted territory– left me shivering.

"I think I should head back home," I started to state. It was at that moment that I saw it; a large grey cloud that just had to have the colors! I became excited, my imagination projecting visions of swirled colors and the smiling faces of the other kids. I glanced at the children to search for their joy; however, I was met with a different reaction: fear. Upon spotting the cloud, three of the kids ran towards the nearest pile of rubble, ducking behind what I can only guess was an old clubhouse. Two other children started screaming, retreating down the path from which we had just come. I was confused, and I tried to get their attention, as to tell them "Don't be afraid! This is normal!" I've seen kids be afraid of the loud noise, but never of the beautiful colors that fireworks created. It was in the middle of the clearing among the dust and the rocks that I saw him: the tallest boy, frozen in place. He must have been paralyzed with joy because once he saw the cloud, he was unable to look away. It had only then occurred to me that the drops of color could land on us, so I ran towards the boy and tried to drag him away from the clearing, tugging on his stiff arm. The smallest girl emerged from behind a rock and pulled me away, leading me back towards her spot.

All of a sudden, a single drop fell from the cloud. I couldn't see any other colors than grey; and then, as if all at once, the sky turned blindingly orange. The air became scorching hot, and the clearing where the boy once stood became a deep, black crater in the earth. There were no dazzling specs, no dancing patterns, and no bright colors. Dark, scorched earth covered the land, and - as if to prove a point - the sky erupted with a bang! Not fully understanding what happened, I burst into tears, the girl beside me silent. I couldn't believe that on my quest to uncover a world of color, I had found one of the world's darkest places. No amount of fireworks could ever drown the crackles & pops that had shaken the earth, yet the world will ignore the dark to prioritize the lights.

The Late Night Contact Shenanigan

By Evelyn Woo (Finalist)

"How are you putting on your contacts now? Getting better?" Mom asked.

"It's only the third day, how could I be used to it?" I replied, annoyed.

I didn't want to sound rude, but I was stressed out enough already over putting them in and taking them out. It was seriously getting on my last nerve, and the more I struggled, the more I dreaded late night and early morning: the times of unceasing, solitary struggle.

But as time never froze, the sky turned pitch dark again and inevitably, I trudged back to the bathroom. Peering into the mirror, my reflection stared back at me apprehensively. Okay, look straight ahead, squeeze the lens out, and it'll all be over in a breeze. Just remember to never blink NO MATTER WHAT for five seconds at the max. Done. It was always so much easier in words than actions.

Patiently, I looked straight forward into my right pupil, pulled my upper eyelid with my left-hand, down my lower eyelid with my right-hand, and gently attempted to squeeze the contact with the tips of my right index finger and thumb. It took a few tries as I had expected, but at last, the lens was out like a bird flying out of the cage it had unwillingly been trapped in.

"Just do the same thing twice, you know you can," I muttered under my breath.

Likewise, using opposite hands, I proceeded to take out the lens from my left eye.

1st attempt: Not even close, but there's always a second.

2nd attempt: Hey, it's fine, you're perfectly fine.

5th attempt: Uhhh...okay, don't panic.

10th attempt: Wait, why isn't it coming out?

15th attempt: What is my problem, seriously???

20th attempt: HOW AM I NOT DYING YET?!?!

Time was passing slowly but definitely steadily, and I was getting extremely anxious. What if I could never pull it out? What was I doing wrong? I wasn't doing anything wrong!!!!

My veins were streams of river spurring out of my pupil, ready to burst out at any second, and my left eye was blood red, I couldn't even tell if the lens was still stuck inside. Was my eye on fire??

More thoughts jumbled in my head, and frustration grew to the point I just wanted to give up everything and go to sleep. Why I was still up at 1:32 AM, I could only blame myself.

Yet, through all of my internal and external struggles for the past hour, I was still alone, fighting a battle that I felt, in fact, somehow knew deep inside, I would never win until...who knew?

I contemplated asking mom for help, but then again, I didn't want to wake her up from her deep sleep and put her into vain as well. I hated myself for not being able to solve a problem I already should've a long time ago, but the harder I tried, the more impossible it was becoming. It was out of my control.

In utter despair, I dragged myself into the master room, crept up to my mom's side of the bed, and tapped on her shoulder for help.

"I can't get my contact out of my eye for some reason!" I whispered in desperation.

She trudged into the bathroom, half-asleep, and peered into my pupil to locate my contact.

"Hey, I don't think it's in your eye," she murmured.

"Wait, what?!?" I cried, in shock. It had to be.

"But I never felt it leaving my eye," I protested, oblivious.

That was impossible.

"Maybe it fell to the ground. It's tiny and transparent; easy to miss," she sighed.

I doubted it, but if her assumption was true, what now? Devastated, I stood watching my last strand of hope dwindling as the apathetic clock ticked away. Mom was crouched down to the floor, wildly searching to find the teeny, bowl-shaped blob that had been causing all the fuss.

"It's here!" She suddenly exclaimed, abruptly ending my train of depressing thoughts. She grabbed my lens from the bathroom corner where the wall and the floor intersected.

"Seriously?" I cried.

It sat on the tip of her index finger, and although I couldn't believe it, I was only profoundly glad that it was found and not in my eyeball. Tiredly, I cleansed the lens with solution, pinched the solution into the case three quarters full, and put the contacts back in where they belonged. Without a moment of hesitation, I flung to my bed and tucked in the covers.

"I've never felt better to be back in bed", I sighed in relief before falling into a deep dream and forgetting all about the mishaps of the night.

The Strange

By Miracle N Etuakwu (Finalist)

Scene: Tokyo, Japan 2014, a shop downtown Tokyo called Kimy?na meaning "The Strange" in Japanese.

"Did you get it?" Ren says in his most quiet voice.

"Well umm...I didn't do it yet." Arimi says nervously.

"I knew you'd be too much of a goody two shoes, never mind I'll do it myself," Ren says calmly and boldly.

"You better have my 60000¥ (Japanese currency) I'll be out in 3 minutes top, unlike you I have experience in this field," he says proudly.

Ren walks into Kimyona the little bell rings as if saying "I know you're here, don't try anything funny." Ren thinks to himself, I need to impress her so what should I "borrow?" He spots a pair of very expensive looking chopsticks. Without thinking he grabs them and starts walking back to the door. "Young man!" The store owner cries. Ren stopped dead in his track. "Ummm y--yea" he stammers.

"Where do you think you're going with my chopsticks" the old man eyes look like they are about to pop out of his head.

"What chopsticks?" Ren said trying to sound clueless.

Next thing he saw, the old man was staring straight at him, right in front of him pulling the chopsticks out of his pocket.

"These," the old man said.

"I--I didn't---" was all that escaped his mouth before Arimi barged into the store.

"It's my fault, I told him to do it," she said breathlessly.

"No, it's not sir, she has nothing to do with this," Ren says.

"I need your parent's number young man." the old man says calmly.

"No need to involve his parents into this, how much do we owe you?" Arimi says nervously.

"7,915,112¥," the old man says angrily.

"What? For a pair of lousy chopsticks!?" Ren blurts out.

"Please calm down sir, I don't have that kind of money, there must be some other way to pay you," Arimi says.

The old man scratches his chin and thinks.

"There is one thing," he said.

"What we'll do anything," Arimi and Ren said in sync.

"We are running low on staff here, as you can see, I'm all I've got." the old man said.

"And, you want us to find you more employees?" Arimi says.

"Not quite, the thing is I don't pay." the old man says.

"What do you mean you don't pay? How are you supposed to run a store if you don't pay your workers!" She yells.

"Well, that's the point young lady. You work for me, for free and I don't tell your parents or the police about any of this." Says the old man.

"Arimi, you don't have to do this, it's my fault I started the bet, so I'll handle it," Ren says sadly.

"Well, you wouldn't be here if I hadn't brought up the 60000¥, so it's my fault," Arimi said.

"You are both equally at fault, so...I'm thinking two employees, is that right?" The old man says with a grimace.

After a month of working for Mr. Matsuura, everything was going decently. Their parents didn't know about it, nor their friends. A few weeks' later things start to get weird, Mr. Matsuura starts giving them odd errands. Last week he made Ren drive two white vans to the middle of nowhere. The day Ren drives van number two. Arimi follows him and stays behind after he leaves, she sees a helicopter land and three men with guns climb out guarding somebody, with a closer look Arimi sees the familiar face of Mr. Matsuura in the middle of the three men in a Rouketsu-Zome Yukata Kimono, which was only meant for O-kane mochi, the rich and wealthy.

She knew this because her father owned one himself. Ren and Arimi begin to get suspicious. Arimi starts doing some snooping around the warehouse and she finds out something shocking. Yuu Matsuura, the owner of Kimy?na, is running an illegal knife and drug distributions in the store's warehouse.

Arimi decides to tell her parents about the whole thing, starting from the beginning. Ren later finds out what Arimi did and tries to confront Mr. Matsuura, but he sees that there are black vans labeled FBI camped out around the front door.

The next day when Ren is quietly sweeping the courtyard, six cops burst through the store's doors, the first one grabs Mr. Matsuura and handcuff him.

"Sir, you are under arrest for an illegal substance and weapon distribution," the cop says while reading him the rest of his rights and loading him into the van.

Another cop comes forth and starts shooting questions at Ren.

"What is your association with this man?" Asked the officer.

Ren told them the whole story, leaving out the part about Arimi being involved. Later that week Ren told Arimi at school that everything is ok; Mr. Matsuura has been arrested, and the officers will not confront their parents.

Arimi told Ren that she already told her parents. "They were mad at first but they understand and will go to the trial with me," Arimi said.

"Oh you heard," Ren says disappointed at himself for not handling it enough.

"And one more thing Ren," Arimi said.

"What now," said Ren

"Your parents want to see you. They are with mine,"Arimi said with a smirk.

The Observer

By Laura Calzada (Finalist)

My body and I have a history together and at times, it is disguised in the form of introversion. I remember a time in my childhood when my skin began to stretch, tearing itself apart, forming bridges of insecurity that dispersed all around my body. I was only 7 years old.

I began to see myself as an outsider to a world that still remained unchanged, it was only now that I wanted to change myself and change every single part of my being. I stared at a reflection in the mirror that appeared to be thinner and smaller; I fell to the beauty expectations and judgements by the voices in my head as well as the voices of my mama, papa, sisters, auntie and my abuelita Every. Single. Day. I would hear. I would listen. I would remember. Never did I forget. Those voices were no longer reminders of how I looked but rather announcements to the world in the form of melancholic symphonies thundering in my head waiting for an action to occur. An action that would find a way to make the voices in my head inaudible and easy to ignore.

I do not remember a time growing up in which I resonated with myself in this body and even less so with my surroundings and the people around me. Every decision I made felt like a huge choice defining my being to others because I believed that my physicality made me a 162 pound defective aloof incapable of becoming indistinguishable in the playground but easily confused for an adult. I wondered of the story behind how I became the pioneer of a body older than my age. I analyzed, visualized how forms of interactions occurred, movements, responses- personality. I admired that. I admired that in people because I did not have that in myself and in many ways, I felt restrained by a self-conscious mind powered by insecurities about my body. It came in the mold of anxiety; it was being behind a glass door where I could see everything and I knew exactly what I needed to do to live in an outside world- interaction- but every time I reached the glass door, I could not get passed it. It was a thin glass door that was not there, because I could still see everything, but it was there in that I could not find a way to interact with the world. It isolated me from the world, like pushing me in a bubble that I could not get out of.

My relationship with my body has changed drastically. Rather than reacting to it and letting it affect all parts of my life, I just witness the presence of my physique, no longer in association with the thoughts and emotions that seemed too had, one day, carry more weight than my body itself. I witness the body that I am in without the resentment of eating and without an impulse to purge, removing my breakfast lunch and dinner. I learned, through meditation, that I have to allow myself reach a focus of high consciousness in order to feel my body for what it is and not as an obstacle blocking me from being comfortable in my own body. And I am reminding myself of this every single day and it is hard but I know it is working.

Deja Vu

By Nicholas Emington (Finalist)

"Xavier, knock that off man! We will never get out of here if you keep giving her that kind of affection!" David remarked amidst a chuckle.

"All right, Alright" Xavier said with a smile on his face. He finished petting the dog and kissed his wife goodbye one last time. As headed outside, he took one last glance at his new blue suburban "cookie cutter" home.

"It's only for a week man! We will be back before she even notices!" David said eagerly. "Come on! I've been waiting a month for this! We never hang out like we used too. Remember the good old times?" he asked, letting out a sigh.

"Yes David. I remember, it's just hard to leave her alone, she's all I have. Well besides you. Lets go." Xavier said as he set his bags in the back of the metallic black chevrolet "El Camino" carefully, ensuring not to scratch it up. "All right, you take first shift Dave", he remarked while attempting to lean his seat backwards. After putting his hat over his face to protect himself from the bright California sun he quietly told himself "I won't ever leave Jen on such notice again. I promise". After repeating that to himself a few times, he closed his eyes and dozed off as David turned onto the barren freeway.

Xavier woke up to David grabbing his shoulder "Hey buddy, where is your insurance at, this one probably won't let me off." Xavier looked in the rearview mirror and deeply groaned as he studied the flashing red and blue lights. Xavier slowly handed him the insurance papers while staring him down. A tall man stepped out of the S.U.V wearing all black. As he walked, his perfectly ironed black pants and shirt made him seem like less of a cop and more like a Secret Service member. He walked up to the passenger side backseat and instructed David to unlock it in a calm and collected voice. David, although confused, made the mistake of pushing forward the switch. As the man bent down and got in, the boys were more than confused. Xavier started "Uh… Sir we are very sorr…"

"Drive. Or Jennifer loses more than your new home." The man slowly said as he pointed a gun to the back of Xaviers seat. Both of the boys heart's sunk in a second. As they glanced at each other, Xavier nodded and David slowly pushed on the gas accelerating to the proper speed.

"If it's money you want, I have it. I can get you anything you want." Xavier said in attempt to break the silence. He slowly took his eyes off the moon and focused back on the man in the back seat using the mirror visor. The man still had his sunglasses on despite the lack of light. He simply grinned and let out a small scoff and then went back to a blank stare.

"Take the next exit." The tall man said sternly. David

struggled to keep his eyes open but out of his love for Xavier and his soon to be family, focused all of his will power into driving. The man then guided them to what he referred to as "The Drop off". As they pulled in, the headlights of the El Camino lit up 3 more S.U.V's. Upon stopping all three men got out of the El Camino and at least a dozen erupted from the mysterious S.U.V's. The tall man walked closer towards the men. Upon whispering something into the last S.U.V, one of the men opened a door. Trying to see through the dark: Xavier moved closer. He burst into tears as he recognized the face.

"Jennifer!" He cried as tears streamed down his face. He tried to run towards her when David grabbed him and turned him around. Then all in one minute but so slow, David's right hand drew back. While his hand sprung towards Xavier, he attempted to dodge it. The hand became so close it was blurry. Then a pain, Xavier closed his eyes bracing. But it was not the pain Xavier expected.

A slight slap on the cheek. "You good Xav?" David said concerned. Xavier nearly jumped out of his bones. "You have been out the whole ride. I was starting to get nervous". Xavier looked behind him. No man. He looked out the window, "Welcome to Hitchhikers Peak, AZ" a sign read. A deep exhale relieved Xaviers worries. He immediately called Jennifer.

"Jennifer!? Honey are you okay?" Xavier thought of explaining the story but figured he would save it for a rainy day. After confirming Jen was okay, Xavier looked at David for a minute and began to chuckle slightly.

"What are you looking at?" David said concerned.

"Nothing. It's just that… you have a really soft punch."

Xavier said with a hint of slyness in his voice.

How You See Me

By Jazzmyne Robinson (Finalist)

Dearest Alethea Cameron Eexs,

I tripped over the last step entering the cafeteria and landed my near fall with a defeated grunt. Lately I've been lacking in basic skills I've had since I was 6, I'm reading words incorrectly, I can't seem to spell, every door is push instead of pull, and now the basic privilege of walking seems to be running away from me. Maybe I'm dying or maybe my brain has become so wrapped up in the beauty of you that the very thought of you has infected me to the point that I can't seem to accomplish anything without thinking of you.

To say that I'm obsessed with you would be an understatement and an exaggeration. While I don't invade your personal privacy and do things like follow you home or to your job, I am exceptionally infatuated with your presence. Your eyes remind me of the hope of spring, your laugh is like a beautiful sonnet and your smell is as intoxicating as it is intriguing and yet, while I am constricted by your beauty, infected by your presence and infatuated, no, intoxicated with your smell, it would pain me to ever let these feelings go.

I want you to fall in love with me. I want you to fall so hard it hurts, I want you to feel this falling fate that is my love for you and I want you to breathe it. I want you to cherish it, because, if for anything that I've wanted, no, needed in my entire life, I need this. I need you. I won't ever admit it to you, especially now. Especially when we've reached a point of comfort, and trust. Now that you are more than just a distant crush, but a person who has cried on my shoulder, slept on my chest and held my hand, if this is all I am to ever receive from you, please, let it be this. Because while I suffer through this agony of watching you and knowing that you have eyes for someone other than me at least this way you'll always, in a way, have me. You rely on me, you trust me. And if I were to pour my heart out to you today, boy would it bleed tomorrow, because my selfish ambition would try and rob you of everything we've ever had and replace it with my pure motive to have you to myself. While you rely on me and trust me to never be so selfish with your kind affection, I am. I can't help it, and I'm sorry but I am.

You stitch my heart back together only to rip it at the seams again. This pain, this constriction of air and continuous gift of anxiety is going to ruin me. Ruin me it will, and yes, I will let it. I will let it because if this is the closest thing to love I will ever get I will stay on this road because while you don't know how enticing you are, I do. I know and I don't think I will ever stop knowing because you have placed an irreversible stamp on my heart and brain that has controlled every decision I've made since the day I met you. Since the day I saw you. Your brown curly locks and award winning smile tied me up and held me hostage, a simple gaze in your eyes and I would pay for my own ransom. You consume me, you consume me and control me and I wouldn't change it for the world.

Your energy is a universal charger, everyone plugs into you and what you're doing. You don't have many friends but you do have a million crowds. A galaxy of acquaintances and each one is in awe of you. You are the sun and we are mere planets gravitating towards your every move. Surrounding you to feed off of your energy. They want your brilliance, your supply of love, respect, honor, truth and wisdom, they want you for the beautiful, intelligent, brave woman you are. You honor your friendships wholeheartedly and if anyone knows you they know this. One hundred and ten percent is given into your relationships all the time. Your love is like a current that picks people up and brings them along on your wonderous path through the wild thing we call life. You love well, you just don't love me.

That is why I am writing this, so that if anything were to ever happen to me you would always have the chance to know how I feel, even if you don't share the same feelings. Consider it as an apology, for all the times I've thought of ruining our friendship just so I can end this ache in my chest and take the risk of actually being able to love you in the way to deserve to be loved. In the way only I can love you, with more than my heart, but also with my time, ears, soul and mind. And before you ask Alethea, no I am not over exaggerating, joking or messing with you in any way. You know better than anyone I only write well when I am in pain, but this pain that I am experiencing is more than tolerable because I am in love with you.' He signed it, it's right here in writing it says, 'Malakai

Daniel Yorks.'"

I squeezed Malakai's hand as he lay lifeless on the hospital bed. While yes, he was alive, he was ultimately unconscious but I had a feeling he knew I was reading this. He was, is, in love with me. I don't deserve him, I barely deserve him as a friend, how could I possibly succeed as a girlfriend? As, I put the letter in my wallet, pulled out my notebook and a piece of paper, I began to write.

Dearest Malakai, I had no idea that that's how you see me...

North, South, East, and Ferdinand

By Lady Ironmill (Finalist)

I once, in my search for the foundation for man's existence, came upon four children called North, South, East, and Ferdinand.

"Hah," you say, "preposterous. What parents would ever name their children in such an absurd fashion. Perhaps they had more sophisticated names such as Joseph and Jemima and Jennifer and Jim, or Samuel and Sarah and Sybil and Sawyer. Even North, South, East, and West would do for some. But not North, South, East, and Ferdinand. What poppycock."

I assure you, I jest not. (And I must warn you, reader, that within this account there will be considerable mention of the name Ferdinand. Discretion advised.)

"Let me guess," I said when I first met the young chap, "Your name is West?"

"No. Ferdinand."

"But," said I in dismay, unsure whether my tongue could handle such enormity, "can I call you 'West'?"

"No," said he. "My name's Ferdinand."

The boy's name, was, indeed, Ferdinand. Apparently his parents were a bit indecisive when the time came for his christening. I could just imagine the exchange:

"What shall we call him?" smiled the mother, knowing full well what the answer would be. Or perhaps not.

"Ferdinand," said the father. (The nurses next door gasped in shock. One fainted.)

"But, dear," the mother replied, trying to negotiate, "all our other children's names-"

"I know good and well what their names are," said he, "and I'm sick of it. I'm tired of asking, 'Where's East?' and expecting to find my little girl when instead I'm given directions to the seaside. I'm tired of hearing, 'North is that way,' and having to explain that I am not looking for north, I am looking for North. It's downright ridiculous. And absolutely no son of mine will be likened to a sunset. I want a plain, sensible, average name for my son, and by golly, Ferdinand it is."

"Dear, you can't be serious," the mother sighed, looking down at her newborn son with great pity. "Ferdinand is hardly a sensible name. What will the other children think of him if we-"

"FERDINAND!" screamed the father (who died a few days later from a sore throat accompanied by a headache).

And that was the end of that.

I couldn't help but feel sorry for the boy. Who wouldn't? Imagine you, only six years into this world, branded with such an intolerable burden. But the child didn't seem to mind the name in the least. In fact, you would've thought he'd been named after the great Caesar himself. Young Ferdinand carried himself with a pride unlike his far more ordinary and practical brother and sisters, wearing his voluminous name like a badge of honor. Some tried calling him shorter, more rational names such as Ferdie or Fred, but the young sir refused all ties to such belittling titles. He was, indeed, a Ferdinand in the midst of adversity.

I carefully marked down the boy's habits in my journal, for who could resist the opportunity to study such a fascinating individual? Granted, it was difficult, given the enormity of the child's title, but it was certainly worth the extra effort. I delved as deeply as I could into the meaning and origin of that fantastic name: Ferdinando, the Spanish and Portuguese translation of old High Germanic terms brought in by the Visigoths, composed of the roots fardi meaning "journey", or alternatively "protection" (i.e. to love, to make peace), and nand meaning "daring, noble, brave," variations being Frederick (Dutch), Ferran (Catalan), Federigo (Italian), and Frigyes (Hungarian). These I brought together painstakingly, searching long and hard for the basis of this subject, and although most had not heard of such absurdity, I managed to find one who was willing to translate into the modern tongue.

To further my investigation of this remarkable lad, I decided that my best course of action would be to accompany the boy to his first day of school the following morning. To my great relief, none of his classmates or assistants seemed to be in any way affected by his presence, and all had perfectly logical names. As the boy's teacher began to call roll, I tried to hide my ecstasy. Here was the chance of a lifetime: to see the interaction between my subject and another human being!

I could tell immediately when the teacher had reached that particular name, for he appeared to be choking on something.

"Fred," he managed finally. I made a note in my journal. The classroom held its breath.

"My name is Ferdinand," said the boy unconcernedly. I, feeling ill with a case of overexposure to bad paternity on the boy's part, offered myself a seat.

After the classroom had collected itself, all continued without calamity. That is, until recess was called, and the class filed outside to enjoy the fresh air.

The object of my study was merrily kicking a round rubber ball back and forth between his playmates, without a care in the world, when suddenly, the ball flew up into the air and careened in the direction of the busy street. Heedless of the danger, the boy jumped up and sprinted to retrieve it.

But even I, the great philosopher and logician of our day (and I blush to say it), succumbed the inevitable. As the child raced out into the street to retrieve his plaything, my mouth opened involuntarily, and the street was filled with the chorus of voices, my own included, all shouting one thing:

"FERDINAND!"

The lad stopped, right there in the middle of the street, his mouth hanging open in dumbstruck awe. It appeared that the shock of hearing his own name had rendered him speechless. Luckily, someone grabbed him before a speeding automobile could further his condition. The boy was sent home that very instant, and to my knowledge, has not been able to speak his given name since (the locals rejoice).

Thus concluded my acquaintance with the four children called North, South, East, and Ferdinand.

Which is why I, Professor Cordelius Oswald Horatio-Agrippa Sylvester de Utterback, PhD, prefer to go by "Phil."

A Redeeming Finale

By Julianna Feit (Finalist)

The snarling glare of light wakes me this morning, eager to surprise me after not conversing for more than a lifetime. I'm shocked by its welcome, the light flashing through my thin eyelids, but I am still as pleasant as I have been for so long. My body is wrapped by the glow and the rocky walls around me are illuminated. I'm happy with the unexpected hello, but I forget myself, and the risks the light has brought floods my mind.

"Who has come to see me?" I groggily, yet assertively, shout to the opening of the cave. "On this, the middle of my sleep, who has come to stare at the old one?"

Without waiting for an answer, I reminisce about my life. How long it has been since the good days. I used to live so freely, soaring the skies above the outside town, feeling the warm breeze slide along my scaly wings. Humans used to fear my call from the night well into the morning, but now some generations have never even heard me, leaving my legacy to rely only on folklore, legends, and tales of the promise of peace I gave to King Emilio so long ago.

"Who goes there?" I shout again, letting my roar carry outside. Finally, a response: rumblings come from the entrance and I see something...

A man!

No, it can't be. I promised the humans to no longer terrorize them in trade for a quiet end for me.

"Why?" I yell to him, although I know he will not understand me. The tongue of my people is far complex, and superior, then that of his people.

He moves closer and I strain to see his scraggly features. I open my eyes more, blinded by the light behind him. He lowers his head in an attempt to show respect, but if he really respected me, he would have never come to my exiled residence.

"What do you want?" I'm already bored of this. I want nothing to do with this soldier, caked in metal, yet still dripping red from inside it. He leaves a sickly trail in my hallway as he limps towards me. I no longer want to look at him, but alas. My old bones don't care enough to tilt my head, so I don't turn away.

After the long struggle to reach me, the man falls at my face. Only now do I notice that he has been clutching something close to his chest. I cannot get a good look, as the thing is swaddled well in golden robes and very tightly gripped by the man.

He begins to speak.

In his crude human language, I cannot bother to understand him. Translating the human speech was hard even all those years ago when I bargained with King Emilio. Now, attempting to listen to this exasperated, pathetic knight would be nearly impossible. So, instead, I close my eyes.

While the man rambles on, a smell fills my cave. Smoke. I open my eyes and see the foggy gas float the outside world. Intrigued by the fire, as dragons often are, I dare my eyes to look further. In the distance, I see flames dancing on the tops of houses, inching ever towards the castle.

Oh, the castle. I remember that, too. Especially when I would frequent the gates of it to frighten the royals in their ornate home. Now, it no longer looks like that. Instead, it looks ramshackle, lowly, attacked.

Now, I hear a cry. A light cry. Soft, yet powerful. I look down to the man, expecting him to be the source, but he lay flat on the ground of my home, motionless.

And yet, I still hear the crying. Where is it coming from? I wonder. I urge my claw to touch the man and push his on his side to investigate.

Now, the crying stops just as I meet its source. The swaddled package the soldier had held so tightly now smiles back at me.

So regal and peaceful, I know what it is. This calm, small human, I know must bear some relation to the calm King Emilio.

This little human shares the spark Emilio once held in

his eyes. The spark of a leader who will undoubtedly start the fire of a new kingdom ready to rise from the ashes.

I have only just met this child, by way of a defenseless soldier whose life was on the brink of a shameful surrender, and yet I know that this child is destined to become a King.

And I know that I am the one who must ensure that fate.

To protect, strengthen, and care for this infant heir will be my final quest. A last hurrah to secure my place in history, to honor my people, and to protect the pride of the people I once loathed.

Peanut Butter Cups

By Jessie Zheng (Finalist)

It was a cold winter night in September when Cash was strolling around the streets before deciding to trail home. Upon approaching the house, he saw the shadow of his Father's body sweep past the window. He took off his grown-out winter coat and walked into his room. Cash lived his life minimally, with no belongings except a bag of caramels. The unexpected frosty nights used to be a problem for Cash but he has learned how to deal with it. He would always go to bed before his Mother comes home. At three a.m, the cycle begins.

"Wake up!" Norah screamed. Cash immediately shot up and ran towards the door. "Get over her you punk. You left the dishes in the sink. You better get to cleaning them before you end up in the dishwasher."

"Yes, Mom." says Cash.

"You know I love you my sweet Son. If you're good, Mommy will buy you lots of those peanut butter cups that you like. Okay?" Norah says.

"Yes, Mom. I- I actually can't eat peanut butter. I'm allergic." says Cash.

Norah looks at Cash with a sharp glare.

The smear on her lips from her lipstick and the broken dark spots of mascara under her eyes gave Cash the hint that he will not be let off easily.

Norah stares at Cash angrily. "You never do anything right!" she shouted. Her words sent shivers through him.

Norah grabbed Cash by the collar and dragged him towards the corner of the room.

"Hitch! Get in here!" Norah screamed as she grabbed the end of a broomstick.

"Geez what he do this time?" Hitch says.

Norah's words were loud and shrewd. "I gave him everything he needs but he still can't do it. He can't! He's not Cash!"

"Honey, don't worry! We ought to teach him." says Hitch.

"No! Mom! I'm s-s-orry! Please!" Cash begged. Fear slithered through every skin and bone on him. He watched the baseball closely as Hitch tosses it back and forth from his hands.

With one swing of an arm, Hitch chucks the baseball towards Cash. It knocked straight into the side of Cash's ear. Missing his head by just a bit. His ear starts to bleed.

"Aw would ya look at that. I missed?" Hitch started laughing.

Norah grabs the broom from the floor and holds it towards Cash.

She started sweeping the floor around Cash excessively. Hitting Cash on the side with the broom as often as she could. The broom pricked at Cash and scraped his arm.

"You need to be swept up, I need to clean this mess!" Norah exclaimed while continuing to stab Cash in the head with the broom.

Cash could not move. He was too weak to fight back but too cold to cry. He was tired. Always tired of the same routine but too scared to leave. He stared at the caramels that he held tightly in his hand.

"This room is a mess." Hitch says as he starts to leave.

Hitch and Norah both walk out the door while the broomstick and baseball laid next to Cash who was left in the dark. Alone, cold, and bleeding out of one ear.

It was the next morning, about 6 hours later, Cash walks out of his room after patching and cleaning up the bleeding from his ear. He hears Norah getting ready to walk out of her room.

"Good morning sweetheart." Norah says while tucking her heels into her shoes and ran out the door to head to work. Cash stares at the figure of Norah walking out of the house.

He begins putting on his winter coat while Hitch walks

into the room.

"Oh you're up. Listen here punk. If you dare remind Norah about what happened last night, I will end you. Got it? Now get out of here since she's gone. I never wanted the real son of hers but at least this fake one I can control." Hitch says.

"You know, I'm tired of living here. Pretending to be Cash, taking all the hits and punishments that led to Cash's death. You ought to think she'd change? After killing her only son? Or at least not forget him. Pick up another child to be him?" Cash chuckles.

"What do you know? Don't act like you have nothing to do with this. You and I both know that you walked into this on your own. When Norah took you home, you wanted to go with her and you led her into thinking you're Cash. I couldn't care enough to tell her the truth but you act all tough now, oh you were the cause to begin with and I can't wait til she ends your life too." Hitch says sternly.

"Unfortunately, Dad. Today is going to be a little different". Cash says as he continues to toss the baseball up and down.

"You really think you'd be able to hurt me with that? You're too weak! You're nothing but a beggar when Norah found you! Norah would never let you get close enough to hurt her either" Hitch laughs.

"Norah's been happily taking the peanut butter cups I make for her. She doesn't have many days left. Simple poison, no biggie." Cash says calmly.

Hitch looks at Cash blankly. "Are you insane? You've

been poisoning her! I knew I should have killed you from the beginning!" Hitch shouted.

Before Hitch let out another word, the ball had already left Cash's hands. With one blow, the ball charged towards Hitch's head and knocked him straight down. Immediately, Cash runs over with a pocket knife and stabs it right into him.

"You taught me well, Dad." Cash says.

Days later, the air was still frosty cold after Cash had ended the lives of his two abusive kidnappers. He's back to where he started, with nothing but a bag of caramels and a small bag of peanut butter cups to keep him company.

Magic Trick

By Ivy Moore (Finalist)

When I was four, maybe six, or something, I was playing on the weathered, flower-pattern couch in front of the TV upstairs. The TV was pretty nice, and it sat nestled in a green wood cabinet that I always thought would break through the floor since the boards creaked when you walked near it. My mom was working in the other room, clacking away on her clunky desktop computer. She had a crusty Obama sticker hanging off it, and I can still feel the dust on the green Windows logo. I used to lean over her shoulder and watch what she was doing when I was bored, or roll around on the creaky guest bed behind her and run my hands over the curly metal bedframe, picking loose threads on the quilt and gazing up at the cowgirl painting above the bed. The quilt is pretty thin now, but the cowgirl still serenely watches you while you sleep.

And you see, I was five and on this very comfortable couch, my mom was working in the other room, and maybe I was waiting for her, or complaining because I was "bored." I was flopping around and playing with this coin, and I don't know if I just had it, or had found it in between the cushions. The cushions were pretty ragged, but not in a lazy, gross way, but because our cat at the time, Jojo, liked to scratch on the couch. We got a new couch that was leather later, and she scratched on it a bit too. When it got really cold in the morning, I would go sit on the leather couch, even if I nearly froze my butt off, and wait for my parents to wake up so we could watch "Wonder Pets" or "Batman", or "Wordgirl", or whatever I liked to watch when I didn't know how to make decisions. I wouldn't ever get a blanket, I would just stare out the window and wait until my dad rolled out of bed and put his on his little rectangle Walmart glasses, the ones he only wore in the morning because he didn't have his contacts on yet. Our TV's guide was blue and white and had pretty blocky text, and I remember skimming around until we found some "Land of the Lost" reruns and would watch those for a while. Or those weird boomerang/wind-up toy commercials on Nickelodeon.

While I was sitting on this ragged couch, I could hear my mom working in the other room and I was playing with this coin. I don't really know how, but I stuck it up my nose. I'm pretty sure I went to my mom and told her, and it seems weird that she wouldn't make me get it out, or maybe I didn't tell her and just said I lost the coin. On second thought, it might have been a bean and she made me get it out. I was never one of those kids who ate too much weird stuff, except one time I was at a playground and I found a plastic Starbucks cup or something, or maybe it was mine and I had finished it. I filled it with the little rocks from the bottom of the playground and took a sip. I swallowed some but then my parents were there. They called to me, I left my venti rock-acchino behind, and ran to the car. We had donut holes. I swallowed those down too.

I gingerly approached my mother and I told her I had something stuck up my nose. It seems strange that she wouldn't immediately force me to snort it out. It's possible I didn't tell her. In fact, let's stick with that: I lied, and/or did not reveal I had stuck something up my nose.

About a year later, I was still in Kindergarten, so maybe I was six by then, my nose really started to itch. I was at school; I went to a Montessori school, and since teaching is practically free range there, I was off doing my own thing, and I got a tissue (thank god). So I had this tissue, and I blew and huffed and puffed because my nose really was hurting now, and in a bloody wad a small Canadian coin emerged. It was so covered in blood that at the time we thought it was a penny, or maybe a button. I went over and showed the assistant and she quietly freaked out. I don't think Montessori training prepares you for a child offering up a wad of blood with some sort of unidentified shape swimming in its midst. She got me a ziplock bag and grabbed the head teacher, who examined it, determined it was a button and called my parents. After I was rushed home and took a nap to "help my nose heal," I got my nose x-rayed and it was determined that there was no damage. It's been years, I don't know where the coin is now. Maybe it's fallen back between the couch cushions.

I said when it happened, I remembered sticking the coin up my nose a year ago. Sitting on the couch, messing around, not thinking. But what I really remembered messing with that day was a bean. But a coin came out of my nose. A coin that had been lodged in my nasal cavity for about a year. Where would I even get a Canadian coin? It really is the most interesting thing that's ever happened to me. The biggest mystery of my life. And it's actually pretty boring. A collection of half-remembered, audio-less snippets that aren't even very funny. I could've snorted it down deeper and stopped breathing, maybe. Or, when I sneezed it out, it could've ripped my nasal tissue, or cracked my cartilage. It could've never come out, just stayed up in there together, a nuisance every time I tried to travel through a metal detector. The moral of the story, the lesson, the takeaway, is that if you stick a bean up your nose, at any point in your life, and even if you snort it out: a year later, a coin will come out of your nose. And you'll realize you're losing your memory.

Granuaile the Tumblr Queen

By Autumn Hill (Finalist)

If there is any member of history who was meant to be brought back to life, it the great Granuaile, Grace O'Malley, Gráinne Mhaol, the Pirate Queen, ruler of the seas and protector of her green Irish coasts. The British saw her only as a brutal pirate, but her people knew better, for they saw her courage, and that her boldness punished the tyranny of British control. Granualie spent her entire, exciting life disobeying the gender roles of her time and thriving on her inherited and improved trading empire. She commanded hundreds of men and a sizable armada of trading ships, all of them ready to do their Queen's bidding. If she were alive today, her career would be precisely the same, a vast kingdom of trade and audacity that refuses to bow before any power.

As such, aside from the Instagrams of her and her wonderful, dedicated crew, tweets stating the superiority of her enterprise, prominent internet trolling, and a booming industry on eBay, her most frequented mobile app would be Tumblr.

There, she would spend her time smack-talking bigots, correcting ignoramuses, conducting an incredible blog filled with her adventures, and discussing feminism pros and misconceptions. Her blog would also include a section on how to become a successful trader, do-and-don'ts of the sea, and forum where she would answer any questions about her craft and livelihood. She would follow any and all blogs that fell along the nautical or Irish theme, as well as encourage and support fellow enterprising traders, male and female alike.

Blue

By Georgia Ringstaff (Finalist and Honorable Mention)

It was testing day, perhaps a prolonged history exam or maybe just a dragged out standardized test. No matter the subject, it was testing day, and that's what made it all the drearier. I, and many other fifth grade students, watched the clock, a rhythmic steady ticking filling the silent, almost stale room. The seconds dragged their feet, the minutes seemed to have forgotten their way, and I, a hungry ten-year-old, eyed the blue candies.

They sat there on her desk—the infamous teacher's desk—with stacks of papers rivaling the Leaning Tower of Pisa. A plastic ziplock bag perched carelessly on a pile of books. Probably a hundred or so small bead-like chocolates encased in an iridescent blue shell made up the contents of the bag. On any other day, I would have disregarded the candies, labeled them as dollar store chocolate—beneath me. For a ten-year-old, I was quite a snob over my sweets. But today was different. I continued examining the ziplock bag, and the treasures it contained. My stomach growled, a low, angry sound, for testing days did not allow snacks to be consumed until every last student had neatly shaded in every last answer bubble. As I watched the final few students finish up their exams and the clock slowly creep towards lunch, my mind envisioned the sweet satisfaction of my teeth crunching down on just one pearly chocolate. I felt my mouth fill with saliva and my stomach grumble.

It was then Ms. Checkely left the classroom, for a brief while, to deliver test sheets to the office. Her swift footsteps quickly grew faint. As it turns out, I was not the only one entranced by the sparkling blue sweets. A few daring kids had already made their way to the bag, and eventually, a crowd was clustered around the candy. We grabbed. We shoved. The ever-obedient, straight-laced students gripped their desks and hissed at us to stop, but we were far too absorbed in the glorious riches awaiting us to care for their remarks. I sat down in my seat quickly, my fist enclosed around a couple sweets I had snatched from the bag. My teeth bit down on the fragile blue shell, and it broke into bits, revealing a melted chocolate core. The pearly candy had a sickening sweetness, and I swallowed it quickly. My mouth was left with an acrid, bitter aftertaste, my hands with bright, blue stains, and my classroom became a thick, suffocating fog. My stomach rejoiced nevertheless.

The ziplock was returned to its throne of books, just moments before the teacher entered the room, its contents reduced to a few lone beads. A notable hush traveled through the class as the click of shoes grew louder. Ms. Checkley appeared in the doorway, scrutinizing a roster, possibly the schedule for our modified day. She appeared rather preoccupied; with a breath of relief, I leaned back, realizing she had not yet uncovered the scene of the crime. A hum of murmuring and squeaking seats settled upon the class, as a sense of normalcy returned. It was almost appalling how it seemed we thought nothing of our misdeed as we headed outside for recess, but if one looked closely enough, they would see through our plastered smiles.

I sat on the playground swings, kicking up clouds of dust with my scuffed up shoes when I heard the news. Ms.Checkely had discovered the class's rotten secret. Playground gossip travels fast, and soon a flurry of murmurs and tense glances permeated the air. It was in that moment, we, the perpetrators, bothered to look at our hands—stained a distinguishable deep blue.

One by one we marched. Every student, criminal or not, trudged to a dusty clearing near the doors of the school building. There Ms. Checkley stood, her arms folded across her chest. The crisp winter air seemed to turn bitter and biting, as she recounted the horror she had found lying on her desk. But we knew all too well what had happened. "Now, fess up," she snapped. Her order was met with silence, for the class knew what was at stake: a month of recess spent indoors, extra laps around the track, or perhaps one of the most prominent fears of any child—the dreaded phone call home. Her voice turned shrill as she once more asked the students to divulge the secret. No one budged. Even the air seemed stagnant. I could almost see Ms. Checkley's voice harden as she said, "Well, I guess we'll do this the difficult way. Everyone, hold out your hands." Shoke and defeat registered through every face, even of those who were innocent. We had been caught blue-handed. As the hands of my peers began to rise into the air, palms face up, my own began to panic. I desperately tried to rub the blue color off, wiping my hands on my shirt and jeans. That's when I felt the crinkle of paper in my left pocket.

I stuck my hand into my pant pocket and pulled a candy wrapper out—a Blue Rasberry Dum Dum, to be exact. Lightbulbs flashed in my brain. As Ms. Checkley made her down the line of students, nearer and nearer to where I stood, I formulated a plan. Seconds later, she stood directly in front of me, her lips taut. Before I could be condemned to stand with the other blue-handed students, I blurted out, "Wait, Ms. Checkley! I was eating a lollipop, and that's why my hands are blue!" Grasping at straws, I shoved the candy wrapper into her hands. A single eyebrow was raised but nothing more, although I'm sure she had not believed my claims. I stood there for a while, dumbfounded by my own extraordinary luck. However, as I turned around to see my fellow students, my friends, huddled in the cold, awaiting their punishment, that ecstatic glee turned icy. A knot formed in my stomach, aching worse than my hunger had almost an hour earlier. The crime had left its mark.

SECTION 2 – TODAY

True Colors

By Jorja Grace Heinkel (2019 Winner)

My home never got much rain. We lived towards the desert, but not like the movie kind of desert, with golden sands and sparkling oases. No sweeping dunes that rose overhead like waves on a raging sea, or anything interesting like that. Instead, we got hot winds nearly year-round, and rain as scarce as coins in a poor man's pocket. The blistering gales would kill my mama's flowers, no matter how much she watered them, and make her cry over each withered petal. Growing up, I got used to the sun always beating down on my little single family home, just like all the others in our neighborhood. The sun always seemed to shine real bright on my folks and I--which was why that one rainy day in November gave me such a surprise.

Rain wasn't near the kind of mystery that snow was (I still have never seen a flake in my life), but it was certainly something worth running out the door in bare feet to see. But when the rain started on that November day, I was already outside. I found myself staring down at my naked feet when I noticed the first drop splash onto the bricks near my toes, and sink in fast like the brick was tryin' to drink it. It wasn't long until the rain put out the shimmering sun that had shone on my house, on me and my family, for the longest time. The sun that nothin' in the world could ever hide from. Yet as I stood there, staring at my bare feet, at the ground, at anythin' but the woman standing in front of me, I saw somethin' in the rain that I'd never seen before. I saw real color.

I thought I knew color; I knew that those bricks at my feet were red in the sunlight, but in those raindrops I realized that sunshiny red ain't red at all. Those bricks were hiding their colors, I thought, like they were afraid of the sun. When that drop fell from the sky and hit that muted, dusty red, it turned as vibrant a red as mama's famous spaghetti sauce. Or red like...red like I don't even know what. Something like I'd never seen before. That was red. Those raindrops kept fallin' and everything they touched showed off the colors they'd been hiding so long from the bright rays of the sun. Their true colors.

I thought I knew green, but those little drops fell on the leaves on my mama's ficus, and it was like Michelangelo had reached down from the sky and dropped one little dot from his paintbrush onto my front yard. The street in front of my house wasn't the same chalky, cracked street that burned my feet every day. After just a few minutes, it looked as slick and black as the River Styx from all those Greek stories my mama would read me. I could imagine it flowing towards me, swarming around my ankles and dragging me with it. At the time I'd hoped it would, though I knew that slick black was still just a road. My breath shook me harder than the wind as the rain kept comin', and that day showed me more colors than I could take. It was that rainy day that showed me the truth that stood before me in the quivering shape of my mama, the truth she'd hidden from the sun.

I didn't want to look at her and I didn't want to see the truth. I wanted the black river to wash me away, so I wouldn't have to listen to my mama tell me she was sorry. Again and again and again.

But I did look at her, finally, and saw that the rain brought out her colors, too. Her hair was usually a bright honey that challenged the sun itself, but in the rain it was strings of brown, like strips of split leather. The rain was all over her, glimmering in her hair, running down her flushed face, pouring from her eyes. She wasn't glowing anymore, like she had for the past few months. Like she had when she started workin' more often, not comin' home until the sun had cooled through most of the night and was gettin' ready to heat up again for the next morning. She had once been bright, so bright, but the rain seemed to take that away. That day, the rain showed me the hidden colors in the bricks and the leaves and the street and in the world, but I had learned a lot more than that. In those raindrops, I'd seen the true colors of my mama as she stood on the driveway, cryin' and apologizin' for not wantin' me anymore. The sun that glowed in her wasn't just for me, because there was another man that loved her, and she loved him more than she ever loved me and my daddy.

Mama's colors were somethin' I'd never seen before and never knew existed, like that brilliant red in the bricks. She wasn't hidin' in the sun anymore, and for the first time, I understood. I'd seen her real colors, even the ones that the sun had tried so desperately to hide. But I still knew that under those strips of leathery hair that hung down in her face, she was still the mama that cried when the flowers died, that glowed like gold every time she smiled. And I could learn to love her true colors just as much as I'd loved the mama before I saw her in the rain.

That rainy day, I learned that even in the desert, life isn't always sunny. Life isn't always...bright. But that's okay, because sometimes you can only see clearly in the rain.

Jack

By Alexander Flint (Finalist and Honorable Mention)

Hello. My name is Jack. About a week ago, while talking with some friends, I was kidnapped. I was thrown into a car and driven away. I yelled and screamed and did all I could do to bring attention to myself but the kidnappers didn't seem to notice. After about ten minutes, the kidnapper stopped the car, grabbed me, and brought me into the house. He kept me in a dark room for days. He gave me no food nor water. Finally, the sadistic man returned to do what he set out to do: torture me until I die. He took out a container of knives, scalpels, and other devices of torture. Suddenly, I felt sharp brutal pains in my head. The room was still very dark and I couldn't exactly see what was going on. The pain was agonizing and I let out a scream that the man didn't seem to acknowledge. He continued his torture with a stab to my stomach. He then preceded to cut chunks of my flesh out. I was crying at this point. The pain was unbearable but my sobs gave the man no pause. He kept cutting for what felt like hours but was likely much less. When he was done cutting, I saw a young boy enter the room. His pure joy at the sight of me was very terrifying. Who were these people?? Did this kid learn from this man that murder and torture is a good thing? Without much time for me to think about it, the man suddenly brought me outside and left me on the porch. My insides felt like they were melting. I saw many people throughout the evening walk up to the house without caring that I was dying right in front of them. My screams of desperation fell on deaf ears as night fell. The last person just left a moment ago and like the others, ignored my screams. This is why Halloween is a very dangerous time of year if you're a pumpkin.

The Pen is Mightier than the Sword

By Pranay Sharma (Finalist)

Three year old me sat in the back of the car quietly tooting away at one of my newly acquired flutes. With a little wheel attached to the top, it was different from anything other kids had. The toy was meant to treat my progressive enunciating problems but over time it would leave a mark on my self-confidence.

Eight years later, I discovered my greatest fear: 6th-grade book reports. I sat in my chair squirming at the thought of presenting A Christmas Carol. Slamming the keyboard, I typed a five-minute essay. I was ready. While I talked just fine, the voice in the back of my mind continued to doubt me. "Pranay, do you want to show us your speech for Thursday?" said my mom. "Sure!" I responded excitedly. I ran to the living room to share it with my family.

I stood there, with the hope of impressing my family. Nonetheless, the room began to feel warmer, and the discomfort started to set in. Vigorously scratching my scalp, I tried to get my larynx to open. I stood there for what felt like thirty minutes; feeling every sweat dribble from my forehead, every squeak coming from my brother's movement, every passing gust of wind from the AC, but not a single word came out of me. I screeched inside my head, willing myself to say something, but I was unsuccessful.

What was wrong with me? Why can't I just talk normally? These questions raged inside my head, and soon it began to torment me constantly. Alongside these thoughts were the constant echoes of laughter from my classmates after every speech, I gave after every sentence misread, and after every word I mispronounced. I was sitting back down from yet another book report, once again spotting several people stifling their laughter from my speech. That was it. The frustration and humiliation that I suffered at the hands of my friends and family made me form a goal: I was not going to let them dictate how I felt, I was going to change. It's this mental fortitude that I found myself, in our high school's speech and debate room, ready to change.

"Take the pen and rotate it horizontally and put it in your mouth." commanded my coach to a room full of debaters. Cheeks stretched, I followed along, placing the pen in between my molars. Everyone started reading and the unified muffling sound gave me strength. I took comfort and started to talk. As I looked around I found myself for the first time, not as the awkward kid who didn't know how to talk but one of many. Slowly practice after practice, hour after hour, I started to feel like part of a larger community, a community that didn't treat me differently because of the way I talked, but as a peer.

Eventually, after losing spit filled pens and forming stronger bonds with my fellow debaters, I saw the improvement in my speaking. I was certain in what I was saying, I used assertive gestures, I held eye contact: I was confident. What used to be terror when talking was replaced with enjoyment as I had conquered what I thought was impossible. While the pen had helped me with enunciating words clearer, I learned to stop doubting myself and to stop letting others perceptions affect me. Constantly listening to my voice with a pen in my mouth allowed me to be comfortable with the way I talked so that no matter who was in front of me, I knew that I could speak eloquently.

I was always taught that the pen was mightier than the sword, but it never occurred to me that the literal application of the metonymy may be just as pertinent in my life. Who knew that holding a pen between my teeth could give me more confidence than brandishing a sword ever could?

Flying Solo

By Leah Thorley (Finalist)

4:00 in the morning; Mom came into my room to coax me out of sleep. I blindly put on the shirt, jeans, and hiking boots I had set out the day before. I shoveled down some breakfast before grabbing my luggage and running to the car. We stopped at HEB to get gas while nervous butterflies fluttered in my stomach. We turned on music and listened to The Beach Boys sing '…that's why God made the radio…' and James Taylor advising us to '…shower the people we love with love…'. We arrived at the airport and my butterflies fluttered a little faster. We went to the desk that I recognized from previous trips to check my luggage and get boarding passes; Mom got a pass to go only to the gate.

We walked to the TSA line and as we wound back and forth we passed a dog, intently smelling every person, almost saying hello but not really. My butterflies calmed a little at the sight. Everything was checked and we moved to our gate. We had time before boarding so we looked around at the other people. There was a pair of tired parents with two energetic children, an older man in a suit talking on a phone, a college-aged girl reading a book, and some twenty other people at the gate. They began A boarding and people lined up to get on. My boarding pass said B though, so I waited. My leg wouldn't stop bouncing and my butterflies were sparrows. Mom looked at me and said that everything would be okay but I was still nervous. It was time for B to board so Mom and I got in line. My sparrows had become eagles. They scanned my ticket and I had to leave Mom at the airport. I said good-bye and turned away, tears welled up in my eyes but there was a strange man behind me and the older man, still on the phone, in front of me; so I swallowed my tears and moved on.

I succeeded in getting a window seat but I was right behind the wing so I couldn't easily see the ground. The sun was only starting to rise. I checked my watch, 5:10, the flight was supposed to leave at 5:30. I settled my stuff and waited. A man walked up and asked me if anyone was sitting in the aisle seat, I told him there wasn't and he sat down. He put away his earbuds and pulled out his phone. Somehow, he and I started talking which put me at ease. He told me about the first time he traveled alone and what happened and we branched out from that and talked about other things. The plane began to move to the launch pad and I couldn't hear anything. I asked to continue our conversation later and he agreed. I put a piece of gum in my mouth and soon after, we took off. We never did continue our conversation.

I knocked around on my computer during the flight, tried to read but stopped for fear of getting motion-sick. My ears popped uncomfortably and the flight attendant gave me some water. I noticed that a boy about my age was wearing a shirt with a Studio C reference on it. This helped my eagles become mildly calm sparrows once more. I ate my snack and looked out the window to watch the sunrise. Over time, the terrain below became drier and my watch read 7:00. We landed a little after that and the man in the aisle seat talked to me a little bit as we waited to exit. As I passed the boy with the shirt in the gate waiting area, I complimented him on it; he was surprised but smiled nonetheless.

The Phoenix Airport was quite busy but I found my gate and sat down. There were some fifty people waiting there, some standing or sitting on the floor. I had an hour or so to wait so I called my family on the flip phone they gave me. I talked to all of my siblings and I was happy to hear their voices. My sparrows had calmed to butterflies. I stood up and went to the bathroom. I waited behind a woman wearing a hijab and a tall African American woman with straight black hair. She smiled at me when our eyes met. After, I went to the gift shop across from my gate and looked at the overpriced magnets and postcards. I bought some fruit snacks and contemplated ordering from Panera but time would not permit. My seat was taken when I went back so I sat on the floor.

They began boarding and I again succeeded in getting a window seat. A man sat in the aisle seat. Eventually, the plane filled up and a woman with a blonde bun sat in the middle seat. We didn't talk until the end of the flight. She was really nice. We landed and got off the plane and now I needed to find my luggage. I felt very important and grownup as I walked through the airport. I went to the luggage bay and found my bags then I had to worry about finding my grandma, who was supposed to pick me up. We found each other; marking my plane travels as over.

I think that you learn a thing or two about yourself when you're with yourself, like how I have an addiction to fruit snacks or that I am weirdly good at solitaire. But most of all you learn about how you view yourself. Glinda the Good Witch once said, "You are capable of more than you know." My parents trusted me to be able to fly by myself, but I didn't think I could until I trusted myself. Many times though, we let our lack of self-trust get in the way of accomplishing our goals. When we brush that doubt aside, we can really let our light shine.

For the Love of Suzanna

By Kaitlyn Gorman (Finalist)

You know how every neighborhood has that one resident who is like a grandma to everyone? Well I was lucky enough to call Suzanna Earl just that. If you've ever met Suzanna, you would know that Suzanna is like the queen of neighborhood grandmas. She organizes all of our block parties and carpools, feeds stray animals, and volunteers regularly at local soup kitchens and animal shelters. Our admiration of Suzanna was outrageous. Of course, this got us all in a little bit of trouble once.

It started off as a joke between a part of our neighborhood and Suzanna, just a harmless "what if". We thought it would be absolutely splendid if she were mayor. Suzanna was flattered, of all people we wanted her? We made posters, banners, pins, signs, commercials, websites, frisbees, water bottles, shirts and even bracelets that said "What Would Suzanna Do?" Everything ran rather smoothly and we found that more than just our neighborhood had a liking for Ms. Suzanna Earl. So by the first Wednesday in November, we were ecstatic to learn that

Suzanna had won the election.

Once Suzanna was officially in office, she made it her mission to fix our streets, build more parks, and get the community more involved in their city. Suzanna made great strides in all of these goals, most within only a month of being mayor. Not only had she built ten parks by the end of April alone, but she also completed a full year's schedule for soup kitchen volunteers in one day. The town of St. Francisville was at its peak, and every other town in Louisiana paled in comparison.

Eventually, tourists wandered over to St. Francisville in hope of seeing some of the magic being done firsthand. Sure they were all coming to see our town, but more importantly, they were coming to see Suzanna. Despite the mass amount of people, we never had an ungodly amount of traffic, we never ran out of food, and the town was never dirty. Everyone did their own part, whether it was by mopping a restaurant's syrup soaked floors in exchange for a meal, washing parked cars or just simply picking up litter at the park.

Sometime in the spring, our town was holding a meeting to discuss the city's condition, but upon meeting we realized it was perfect. It was then suggested that maybe Suzanna move onto bigger and better things. We loved Suzanna but it just wasn't right to hoard her all to ourselves. So Suzanna Earl ran for president.

Suzanna won the election and the state of Louisiana lit up. For weeks we had a party or parade every day. The streets of Louisiana were covered in a constant layer of confetti and candy for nearly three months! As a result, one of Suzanna's first acts as president was to create a recycling and anti-littering program that took care of the mounds of trash that had accumulated from our parades. The program was such a success that eventually nearly all of the country's forests were even cleared out, which ultimately helped increase our wildlife population. Scientists studying global warming and species extinction presented Suzanna with statistics to prove later the progress we were making.

One day Suzanna was basking in all her glory and the sunshine. Surely no one else could have made so much progress in such a short amount of time and yet she didn't feel appreciated. Looking back we all should have acknowledged what Suzanna was doing for us and how ungrateful we were acting for it. It doesn't matter how small or simple it is, every action deserves something; even if it is only a simple "thanks". As a result, Suzanna began to simply disintegrate. She saw no point in doing anything more for people who didn't seem to care for her.

It started innocent enough, having just a few more festivals and celebrations, you know all that jazz. Then Suzanna decided that there really was no need for "regular" days, everything was already perfect and no work truly needed to be done other than simple maintenance. So Suzanna made every day a holiday, literally. May 14th was National Pancake Day; we glazed the streets and sidewalks with syrup and butter and made pancakes bigger than any A-list celebrities' mansion. November 7th was National Orange Day (Suzanna's birthday and favorite color might I add) which resulted in monsterous orange spotlights being shot up into the sky, casting an orange tint over the entire country. We had orange balloons, streamers, cake, pop and of course just plain oranges strewn anywhere and everywhere; from the tops of skyscrapers to the sewer grates in the subway stations. Eventually absolutely nothing was being done. So we decided to talk to Suzanna, as Suzanna's original neighbors and the reason why she was appointed as president it seemed like if anyone should it was us. So we trekked over to the -once white and now bright green- house. It took us awhile to get passed the kissing lizards and the swarm of polka dotted butterflies, but eventually we found the office.

After waiting for an eternity, Suzanna walked into her office and stared at us. We began telling her how we felt and how worried we were. Suzanna broke down in tears, wailing that for a long time she felt like she was doing all this work for nothing, that no one cared for her and all she wanted was a simple thank you. I'll never forget the looks on everyone's faces, we had failed the woman who had done everything for us and we didn't even know it! Suzanna announced later that week that she was done being president and came back home. She didn't throw any more parties or plan anything for the community. While Suzanna will always be an inspiration to us all, it's time for us to do our own work, no matter how small the action required is.

A Familiar Face

By Acsa Hemandez (Finalist)

I looked in the mirror in absolute disgust. Every time I looked at myself such dissatisfaction came over me. I wonder when the last time was I just passed a mirror and didn't stop to judge what I saw. Picking out every single flaw. The person staring at me felt so distant. She had straight long brown hair, with light brown eyes, small lips, and big eyes. Was this me? I touched my cheek lightly, and then reached for the mirror wanting to see how real she truly was. But as I placed my hand in the mirror, my fingers slipped through it. I quickly pulled back and gasped. What was that? Was I hallucinating? I shook my head and exited the bathroom thinking maybe I have been looking in the mirror way too much.

The next morning, I kept changing clothes, nothing looked good on me. Nothing hid my insecurities. My mom knocked and slowly peeked into my room. "What's wrong? Why aren't you ready for school yet?" she asked me. I gave her no answer as I changed into my pajamas, and when I was finally under my bed covers I said "I don't feel so good today, I think I'm staying home" I knew my mom wasn't buying it, she knew very well how bad my insecurities got to me. Sometimes I didn't even want to go out because I felt too embarrassed about my body. It just never got so bad to the point I had to miss school. I could still feel her standing by the door and looking at me until she finally said "I hope you feel better Elle, call me if you need me. I'll be home by 6:00pm"

The moment I heard her close the door, I broke down. I never understood why I couldn't find comfort in my own skin. Each day it felt like I was able to breathe less.

I woke up, and when I checked the time it was 1pm. I decided to get up and eat something because I at least could do that for myself. I walked past my mirror, and I saw a lady sitting in a chair with her back turned to me. I instantly looked back to my mirror to see what I had just seen, was I hallucinating again? But when I turned back, I saw nothing. I could have sworn I had seen a lady sitting in front of a desk, in what looked like an office. Then, a thought sparked my head. I slowly walked towards the mirror and placed my hand on it, my fingers slipped through it. I gasped. I tried this once again, but this time my whole hand passed through the mirror. As I pushed myself forward, I had passed through the mirror and I was standing in front of that lady I had seen. She had short brown hair, wore a yellow long sleeve shirt, and jean pants.

"Hello? What is this place? Am I dreaming?"

Immediately she turned around. She seemed to be in her 20's. She smiled, "I wasn't expecting you to be the one to come to me, but I guess I got lucky"

I had so many questions rushing through my head, "who are you?" is all that came out.

"Why don't we eat first, and then I'll explain?" she smiled and walked out of the room, I felt like I could trust her.

"I work as a Mechanical engineer. We have been trying out this new machine where it works as a time machine"

I almost choked on my words, "a time machine?!"

"A time machine. Individuals must place this little machine on top of their mirrors, set the date they want to go to, and they can pass through the mirror. There is so much to explain about the science behind it but that is the basics of it"

"So, does that mean you're future me?"

"You catch on quick"

"But wait, why would you want to see me? Why would you want to come back to this age?"

"Because this is where it all started"

"What started?"

Future Elle said, "Where the beginning of everything began. At age 14 is when I remember I became so deeply sad with who I was. I was so angry with myself, and it impacted me negatively later in my life. My insecurities are what limited me from so many things. I thought maybe I could speak to you for a moment, and give you some advice"

We spoke what felt like hours. We spoke of what we had accomplished over the years, and how we overcame many obstacles. Yet, I could see her sitting in front of me full of hope.

When it was time to go and we were standing in front of the mirror, future Elle took my hand. "I hope you realize what I didn't when I was your age"

A worry raised in me "aren't you afraid that this may change the future?" She smiled and said, "I have hope that I am meant to have a bright future, maybe it won't look like this exactly, but I hope it will be bright"

I promised myself I would be like her, hopeful.

I turned to the mirror and took a step forward.

I woke up to my mom calling my name from the kitchen. My mom came into the room and said, "Hey sweetheart, what do you say if we go out for dinner?" I smiled, "I'll be ready in a few minutes"

I walked to my mirror and everything felt normal until I realized, I felt a sense of familiarity when I saw myself. As if I knew who I was looking at. I looked at a yellow long sleeve shirt that was laying on the floor, I put it on. And when I looked into the mirror, I smiled. Yellow looked good on me.

Dog Days

By Mickilina Volpi (Finalist)

Sarah Greenwood rolls over and falls out of bed with a thunk. On the way down, her head hits the end table and a throbbing headache develops. "Ouch!" She rubs her head and scrunches up her messy hair.

She sits up on the floor and looks at the alarm clock in a blurry daze. 7:33 flashes in big red numbers.

"No. That's not possible. Why didn't the alarm go off?" Sarah quickly jumps up and stubs her toe on the bed stand as she races for the bathroom. "I'm late!"

For 15 minutes, Sarah is an Olympic athlete doing wind sprints around her apartment. She brushes her teeth, makes an instant coffee to rinse her mouth, and rips three panty hose before deciding on pants instead. Finally, she hurries out the door as she puts on her black business pumps. Racing down the three flights of stairs, she nearly knocks over Mr. Overton who is walking his miniature poodle, nearly crushing the little thing.

"Sorry, Doodle!" she yells at the small dog.

"Slow down Sarah, you're gonna miss out on life always racing around!" Mr. Overton yells at her back as she waves and rushes down the street to the bus stop.

Sarah makes it to the 700 bus stop and gets the driver's attention before he leaves making it at the last second. She walks to the back of the bus, and on the way there, her heel breaks, and she stumbles onto the floor, spilling her purse across the aisle.

"Slow down there, miss. Are you okay?" An older man on the side of her asks as he helps her get up. A young high schooler helps her with collecting her purse contents.

"Just peachy. Thanks." She continues on to the back of the bus and sits in the last spot. The bus gets stuffy, so she reaches over and pulls the window down. A memory of her childhood goes off like a lightbulb.

Driving down the back roads with the hand rotating windows put down all the way. Sarah reached her hand out the window and moved it to the fluid motions of the wind. She blasted the radio, not really caring about what song was playing, but more caring about the feeling. The feeling of freedom. The feeling of escape.

What happened? I miss those days. Sarah thinks to herself.

The long nights outside, under the blanket of the stars, in the bright light of the full moon. She listened to the frogs hum the songs to the ones they love. Her dad built the bonfire, and she watched each spark soar into the night sky and waited until the darkness engulfs each and every ember. Her family roasted the giant marshmallows with long sticks, and she would laugh when Ma sets her marshmallow on fire and waited till the whole thing was completely burned.

She also used to catch lightning bugs in mason jars with her friends. They jumped over the white picket fence into her neighbor's yard, and would shush each other and watch to make sure the house lights didn't come on. They ran through the vast meadows playing tag in the dark of the night. They never knew that beauty could still be found in the darkness.

But as fast as it came, summer was gone. Freedom was taken away, and the beauty and warmth of summer disappeared. The bone-rattling chill of winter took its place. A new and unpleasant memories overtook Sarah.

Her dad's business went under. Both of her parents had to get multiple jobs, and all they did was work, work, work. Sarah would get home from school and was greeted by emptiness. She never had any help on homework, she would make microwave dinners, and she would sit alone at the dining room table that was meant for three. Her parents worked the long hours, and they cared more about their job than their only daughter. She learned that the only way to thrive in this world was to fend for herself. No one was there to support her. Life was meant to be successful, not to be enjoyed.

Sarah leaned back against the bus seat. I sure did follow in my parents footsteps. Sarah thought to herself. If only we could take our childhood with us to the real world.

The bus stops a block from her work, and she hurriedly limps to her building.

She anxiously waits for the elevator in the lobby, then when it comes she quickly dives into it hitting the 25th floor just as another worker races to get on. Sarah apologizes with her eyes, and taps her watch.

As the elevator dings, she hurries up and finds her boss Harold standing at the reception desk. Sarah freezes as Harold looks up at her and then looks at his watch, surprised. A thousand excuses appear in her head, but Harold beats her to the punch.

"You're early." Harold smiles.

"What do you mean?"

Her boss laughs. "Sarah, love the initiative. Way to start off the week working hard!"

Sarah just nods not sure what is going on.

"Sarah." He smiles and shakes his head back and forth. "Loosen up a little. Not everything has to be so stoic and serious all the time. You should have some fun. Enjoy life. You can't take anything with you but your experiences!" Harold pats her on the back and walks to his office.

Sarah heads over to her desk and looks at her cell phone for the first time. She laughs at herself. "Thank God for Daylight Savings."

A Stop in Time

By Michael Kelly (Finalist)

I shut the door and walk down the front steps of my house. The cul-de-sac I live in is positioned more or less within the opening of a forest, making it seem hidden from the rest of the world. The trees obscure the majority of the morning sky view, creating a faint hue of orange. A sharp chill rasps through the morning air. The sound of rustling leaves overwhelm me, sounding like an invisible, yet vast ocean. Leaves of various warm shades silently drift down from above.

Stopping momentarily, I shiver.

"Another cold day..." I mutter to myself, looking upward at the swirl of leaves raining upon me. I slowly draw in a deep breath of air, filling my lungs with a prickly sensation. The air had a distinct nature taste to it--very piney. The scenery may have seemed dreamlike to some; however, after reliving this exact moment every morning for the past two months, it's beauty became practically numb to me. Once I finished briefly taking in my surroundings, I continue to traverse through the forest foliage, creating audible crunches and snaps in the process.

It was Autumn. Though, It didn't quite feel like it.

To me, it was a Monday, the start of yet another long five day school week. Who could blame me? School often occupies the thoughts of a student. There are tests to do, friends to see, grades to make, and parents to please. Doing this day in and day out for years can weigh heavily on one's mind. Because of this, I wasn't able to appreciate the simple things right in front of me.

Not until today, at least.

The wind faintly whistled as it gently brushed against my cool face, as if to tempt me to go home and slip back under my warm bed covers. The thought of this tired me. Along with the monotonous pounding of my footsteps against the solid asphalt, reverberating throughout the desolate area. Along with the warmth of my breath, freezing into a hazy mist and landing softly on my slightly rose checks. Along with the view of the reddish sun, lazily making its way over the distant mountains.

Leaves scrape against the old sidewalk, catching more momentum as they tumble downward.

Before I knew it, I reached my destination: a stop sign stationed on top of a large hill.

There was a girl, whose name I did not know. She had hair as orange as the leaves around her, melting seamlessly into the dawn sky. She was silent, like I, though not due to the dread of another long week. She was always the first at the bus stop, making her seem like a manifestation of the hill itself--a guardian of some sort. Though I do appreciate her near angelic features, this is not the reason why I find her so fascinating. She seems to be as quiet as I and yet, looks so much more...enthralled.

But enthralled with what?

Was she contemplating the hardships of the week as I, the only difference being a tone of optimism? Did she enjoy the cold? Why was she smiling with that luminous, bright grin? What is there to laugh at, and why? Was she mocking me? Was she--

"Try smiling once in a while, it helps." The girl says suddenly, without warning.

I freeze, utterly petrified. Had I outwardly showed some sign of what I was thinking without notice? Her remark was so out of left field that it took me a few seconds to process.

"Why smile when there's nothing to smile about?" I reply, slowly.

A pause.

Feeling like I needed more explanation to my response, I continue, "It's cold, I'm tired, the day hasn't even started yet..."

The girl turned to me with an all-encompassing smile, not even batting an eye. "No reason to smile? Look around you, and tell me what you see."

Dumbfounded, I follow as she instructed. "I see...trees,

the sky, birds..."

After deeming the task pointless, I gave up shortly after I began. Recognizing my resignation, she continues, "Now, look at the same things again, but this time with your heart."

"--?"

I look at her, then back to my surroundings. What did she mean by this? Is this a play on words? Have I missed something? What could she possibly--

Ah.

Now I see.

It wasn't a matter of what was there and what was not. Whether she saw and what I saw. Whether it was a Monday or a Sunday.

It was how I perceived it to be.

The once bland trees had now transformed into a beautiful coalition of reds, yellows, and oranges, like apples ripe for the picking. The once silent, barren sky now a large canvas overlayed with a warm, majestic pallet as the sun crept from the depths of the horizon, arising from its slumber. And the birds... The birds were singing! Right now, in this moment, they were not winged-rats that chirped indefinitely whose sole purpose was to disturb my tranquility. They now sung songs one would only hear upon their to arrival the gates of heaven itself.

The sight was tremendous, a true spectacle.

I fix my gaze back at the girl, finding myself back in my solitary silence. Only this time, it was not prompted by dread.

This was a silence of awe. There was no need for an exchange of words to express my newly found realization, for my growing smile said it all.

The girl, witnessing this, shook her head nonchalantly as she set her gaze behind us, signaling that our transit had arrived. The thunderous roar of the bus became less and less distant as it approached, screeching to a halt at the stop sign. The glass doors opened, and after taking a final glance around me, I enter the vessel. The double doors hissed shut, and we made our decent downhill.

Then time went on, much like that dawn.

A Rainy Day

By Megan Lovejoy (Finalist)

Soft rain patters on the windows. The smell of spring fills the air. Flowers are blooming- hopefully not just to be drowned by the oncoming storm.

It looks so peaceful out there...

"Come outside with me." I smile, love filling my eyes as I look at him.

Without hesitation, he stands up, walking to me happily.

"We can walk in the woods- It'll be wonderful!" A grin fills my face, and I open the door for him to follow me. I'm sure to grab my keys, wouldn't want to get locked out like last time.

He follows, not questioning my strange habit of going outside whenever it rains. He never objects to something that will make me happy.

"You know, I'm so glad you always are just... there for

me. You never try to force me to be someone I'm not, you're always there whenever I need to just talk... You're a lot better than anyone else I spend time with." I let the words flow out of my mouth like a waterfall of praise, and he gives me a happy, knowing look.

We walk all the way into the woods, side by side. We finally get to our spot- an open section, flowers dotted around, and enough trees nearby that we can stay mostly out of the rain.

"What would I do without you?" I ask, sighing.

He doesn't respond, but leans on me instead. He always reminds me that he needs me almost as much as I need him...

"You know, someday, we'll both die, and everyone we've ever loved will die, and life itself will cease to exist on the earth. And there's nothing we can do to change it..." I often get like this. Drifting into questioning reality... He always brings me back though.

He looks at me with a pleading look, silently saying 'please don't worry about all that.' It's nice, having him. Everyone else has left, or started to make fun of me, or pushed me away. Not him. He was always there. Hopefully he'll continue to be.

"You're right- I shouldn't worry. Live life as it comes." I smile again, watching the rain start to fall more and more. Soon we'll have to go inside... Oh well.

A few minutes later, as he follows me back to our house, I smile yet again, and think to myself: "Having a dog as a best friend is great."

To Have a Purpose

By Diana Farhat (Finalist)

I am about to turn nine years old and I have to wear a scarf around my head. My over-protective yet positive mother said "it is part of your religion, you must wear the hijab in order to obey God's rules", in an elaborative tone. The thought of me putting on a type of shawl got me thinking how the intense sun will make me nothing but burn my body and the feeling of later getting hurt; also known as bullying.

I am now nine years old and I am wearing the hijab. Scared, frightened, and nervous I was upon attending my first day of school in the fifth grade. My situation on campus went a little bit like this: keeping my head down at all times after passing the roaming hallways and classrooms, not being completely an active participant in class as I usually am, and the questioning of my fellow classmates asking me what that cloth was on my head. Embarrassed and self-conscience I was, I was just not ready to tell them why. I cannot handle what people will think of me, either if I am just weird or unattractively disgusting by wearing such a thing. I cannot just tell them because it is part of my religion, my thoughts called to my blushing self-esteem. Everyone has tons of religions in school, and here I am, the loner one having the only religion that deals with wearing the hijab.

If only they understood, if only they knew the struggle on wearing this during the hot flaming and smoldering days, if only.

Presently, I have been in my own imaginative and little world. I have been distant from anyone and everything. From coming back straight from school, studying and doing my daily homework assignments, and pretending to be happy in front of my mother. Truth is, my mother thinks I have been satisfied and happy with the experience of wearing the hijab to school. I cannot be honest if I am this sad. The point is, I am facing depression, I wrote down in my thick and descriptive journal.

One passing morning, I was writing nonstop on my journal. There was so many things in my mind; for instance, the constant rhythm on how my life would be in the next ten years, how will my friends and mother feel about this, how I will eventually move on into reality than my cheerful past. As the movement of my hand was in a fast pace, I wrote how difficult and tough it is being the only child with a single mother in a household, while still grieving on my father's death. This has brought attention as to why my mother is overly protective of me, she wants to take care of me the way daddy has done to me. That's just it, I thought momentarily, I need to continue the legacy of my father and become as mindful as he once was. "It all takes time", I said aloud with no awareness in the room.

It has been three years, I am now in the eighth grade. I

am a big girl now, no matter the age and no matter the hijab, I am a strong and independent woman. I am now in control of my conscience and know that people are not as negative as negative when the meaning is out. My experience on campus went a little like this: I finally stood on my big two feet, rolled up my sleeves, and announced to my friends that "God has put me in this world to convey the modest presence of the hijab; a scarf worn to represent the purity of women and a strong legacy to God's rules and the interpretation of the mighty religion: Islam", told in my bravest attitude. Silence followed the room and here, I was happy I let out my frightful feelings and did not care whether they had negative comments to say about me wearing the hijab. Instead, my classmates and other people I did not recognize or know were very interested in my religion and wanted to know even more than the hijab. I began to explain...

Home sweet home, and what a beautiful and educative day it was at school. I ran up to my mother and said "I love you" in a soothing and admirable resonance.

Nobody Stays

By Kimberly Lau (Finalist and Honorable Mention)

Some people have lots of friends? I have Nobody.

Why? It's simple. Nobody can be trusted.

Everybody leaves eventually. Nobody stays.

My mom died when I was really young and my dad was never around, so my older brother Danny raised me.

He helped me with homework and he listened to my stories He always laughed at my jokes and when he smiled his face would light up, dimples would appear, and I knew everything would be okay. He had red hair and freckles, and I told him wanted to marry someone just like him when I got older. He laughed when I told him that. I laughed too. I told him everything because I knew he would listen. Danny was my best friend.

But on my eleventh birthday, he collapsed, and my

world started to fall apart.

One minute we were eating cake, and the next minute he was on the ground. He wasn't crying or sad, but he wasn't breathing or moving either, and I didn't know what was happening, so... I just froze.

Mrs. Henderson, one of my neighbors, called for an ambulance since my dad wasn't around. The hospital told us that Danny had developed malignant mesothelioma. I didn't know what that meant.

"I'm just sick," Danny explained, "So I'm getting extra help."

"When are you gonna get better?" I would ask.

" ... I don't know."

Months went by, and he still hadn't recovered. The cancer was growing, and the doctors hadn't been able to stop it yet. He started wearing a beanie, and I couldn't see his bright red hair anymore. Danny told me that he cut it short because he wanted a change, but I knew he would never give up his hair like that.

"Danny," I asked him once, "Are you gonna leave me?"

"Katie... I don't want to, but everybody has to go eventually. Nobody can stay forever."

"Then... can you be Nobody?"

He laughed slightly and simply said, "There is someone out there who will love you more than anybody else. You just have to look for them."

"But…" I hesitated, "Don't I have you?"

"You'll find someone even better than me."

"Really?"

"Yep," he smiled warmly, dimples showing, "I promise. One day, you'll run into someone perfect."

I started going to school again after that. I tried looking for the Someone he told me about, but I couldn't find them.

My classmates teased me, but I didn't give up. I wanted to find Someone.

I didn't want Danny to worry about me, so I didn't tell him about the mean kids at school. I stopped visiting him for a while since I didn't want to bother him.

Three weeks passed.

It was a Thursday. It was a picture perfect spring Thursday. Birds chirped, flowers blossomed, and the sun shone brightly.

On days like this I would usually ride my bike with Danny, so I decided to visit him. I figured it would be fine to talk to him about riding bikes. That shouldn't bother him. I would tell him some jokes, and we'd have fun together.

I got Mrs. Henderson to drive me down to the hospital, but Danny wasn't there. The doctors had to rush him into surgery earlier because his lungs filled up with fluid or something. Either way, it didn't work. Danny never told anyone that he was hurting, so they weren't able to help him in time.

Mrs. Henderson offered to stay with me until my dad came, which happened to be all day.

When Dad finally showed up, he told me that he made arrangements for me to live with my Aunt Clarice. I didn't even know I had an aunt named Clarice.

I didn't fight against it. I packed my clothes and pictures of me and Danny. Then I left. I left everything I knew. It was like the world I grew up in suddenly blinked out of existence.

Aunt Clarice welcomed me into her home but I didn't pay much attention. Danny was gone. Everything I had was gone.

"Nobody can stay forever," he told me. So... all I had to do was find Nobody, right? Then I'd never be alone. Nobody wouldn't leave me.

I cried out for help... and Nobody came.

Everything I knew disappeared. Everybody leaves eventually, but Nobody stays.

Nobody would help me now.

Nobody would be my friend.

I started going to school again, and I knew I would never meet Someone. Nobody told me Someone wasn't real, and Nobody always tells the truth.

Nobody helped me with my homework. Nobody listened to my stories. Nobody laughed at my jokes.

Everybody ignored me, but Nobody always listened.

I knew that Nobody cared, because Nobody always came.

I trusted Nobody, because Nobody was always there for me.

On the first day of my senior year of high school, I asked Nobody if I should wear blue or purple. Nobody told me to wear purple, so I did. I had trouble finding my science class, so Nobody found a map for me.

When I walked into the classroom, I saw a boy with red hair. He was sitting in the back row reading a book. Nobody told me to ignore him, but I didn't listen.

As I moved closer to him, I realized he had a light dusting of freckles on his cheeks.

Nobody told me to walk away. Nobody told me I shouldn't talk to him. Nobody told me to ignore him. Nobody told me that everybody leaves eventually.

I stopped listening.

I looked at this boy, this boy that looked so familiar yet so different, and I knew I couldn't stay silent anymore.

"Hey, umm.." I started awkwardly. He glanced up from his book briefly.

"Yeah?"

"Are... are you Someone?"

He looked back at me, confused. Putting his book down, he gave me a crooked smile.

"I guess so," he said, dimples playing at the corners of his mouth. "Do you need something?"

The Mess

By Kathryn Howard (Finalist)

Tia Olsen

It was the early in the morning. Too early. I woke up in a cold sweat, breathing hard. I didn't know exactly what I had startled me, but a feeling of dread seemed to be spreading through me, like ice traveling through my veins, cutting me from the inside. Knowing I wouldn't be able to fall back asleep, I stood up in the dark and felt around for my clothes, quickly got dressed, and then perched on the edge of my bed. I glanced around uneasily. I walked over to bathroom to brush my teeth, and as soon as I flipped that light switched, my life flipped upside down as well. Written in cryptic, red letters on my mirror were the words, "Help me,"

I ran out of my room, and into my dad's room only to find that he had worked the night shift last night, and probably wouldn't be home until 8, which was three hours away. My older brother was most likely passed out on the couch, and I knew he was going to be no help at all. I crept back out into the hall, and decided to check all the doors. I quickly glanced around. Front door? Locked. Back door? Locked. Garage door? Locked. My house was small enough I could see them all from the place I was standing. Except for the basement. But there was no way anyone was in the basement. My dad always kept it padlocked. He was paranoid that we were going to go down there and mess up his model trains, or whatever weird hobby he was into.

I grabbed my cell phone from my pocket, and dialed 911, but then paused. Would the police really believe or care that a 15 year old had something written on her mirror? What was I going to say to them? I couldn't exactly report a break in. I tentatively crept back into my room, jumped into my bed, and buried myself under the covers. I didn't sleep.

Finally, as the sun began to creep up from behind the mountains, and I could hear the cacophony of my obnoxious brother, Jonathan. banging around pots and pans making breakfast. I felt safe. For now at least. Maybe Johnathan, or one of his stupid friends had done it as a prank. That's it, I thought. That had to be it. I walked into the kitchen, and poured myself a bowl of Fruity Pebbles.

"Tia get in the car, we are leaving!" My brother yelled walking into the garage. He started honking like crazy.

"Shut up! I'm coming!" I yelled slamming the door behind me.

As I got to school, I hastily grabbed my math notebook. I couldn't be late for class again, or Mrs. Riley was going to kill me.

As I sat down in my seat and Mrs. Riley started on her monotone lecture about the cell cycle, I began turning over the events of the morning in my mind. It could be my brother pulling a prank, but honestly, he's just too lazy. He wouldn't do that when he could me making out with some girl. I closed my eyes suddenly overwhelmed by everything that was happening.

The worst part was that I had no one to talk to about it. I didn't really have any friends, my mom has passed away, so my dad has been working all sorts of jobs with weird hours, and is never really around. My brother, well, he's just a whole other story on his own.

During each class, the clock almost seemed to tick backwards. Each tick seemed to whisper to me that I would never escape this class. Every bell ring, locker slam, and toilet flush, made me jump. By the end of the day, I had decided that it had to be someone playing a practical joke on me, or even more likely, I had imagined it all.

I got home, double checked that all the doors were locked, grabbed myself some chips and cookies, changed into sweats, and parked myself in front of the T.V. It wasn't until I was sitting down, watching T.V, that I realized how tired I was. I started to nod off.

I was woken with a start when I heard the beeping of the microwave. I opened my eyes to see that it was dark outside. It was my dad fixing himself a microwave burrito.

"Hey Dad,"

"Hi Sweetie, how was your day?" I hesitated for a moment, then replied

"Fine, how was yours?"

"Good. Just so you know I'm working late tomorrow, so you are on your own for dinner, alright kiddo?"

"Ok," I replied the disappointment in my voice, but my dad too clueless to hear it. I started mindlessly scrolling on my phone because if I looked at him again, I might cry.

"Also, the cleaning lady is coming over tomorrow for the monthly clean, so go see a movie or something after school. I'll give you some cash,"

"Thanks," I mumbled without looking up

I made myself a PB and J, told my dad goodnight, and dragged myself to bed. I didn't change into my pajamas, or even brush my teeth, I was too tired to deal with what I might to find on my mirror.

Mariah

As a cleaning lady, you learn things. You can learn so much about someone's life by cleaning up their messes. I've learned Mr. and Mrs. Hansen aren't the happiest couple. Divorce paper clutter the office, dried mascara on her pillowcase, bedding on the couch. I've learned Mrs. Cotter is going through a midlife crisis. Travel brochures litter her kitchen counter, a new car in the garage, a box of hair dye in the trash. But some people hold more dangerous secrets. I just spent the last hour mopping up blood in Mr. Olsen's basement.

Winter Is A Wonderland

By Paige Weinsein (Finalist)

The breeze of the cold winter morning pushed the curtains aside as the sun brightly sparkled through the little crack the breeze had so gently created. The sun shined on my eyes, not caring at all that I was trying to sleep. My mother, already awake, got up from where she was sitting, kissed me on the cheek, and being as quiet as a mouse, pulled the curtains closed. I smiled unaware that I was doing so and I quickly fell back into my dreams where unicorns were real and there was a pot of gold at the end of every rainbow.

I woke again, but this time to the pleasant smell of pancakes as I was snuggled warmly in my blanket. I crawled out of the comfort of my bed to my bare feet touching the cold wooden floor. I walked over to my window where I slowly pushed it close, but not before admiring the smell of the winter air. My eyes quickly shot over to the house across the street as I noticed the sun bothering another sleeping family. The brightness from the sun was almost blinding, but the sight of snow quickly made me forget about how much the sun burned my eyes.

I turned away from the window, pulled out a pair of fuzzy socks and put them on my cold feet. I walked down the stairs to the sight of my mom listening to The Beatles, dancing, and making my favorite breakfast...chocolate chip pancakes. She glanced at me, smiled and went back to dancing. I laughed and joined in on the dancing. It was the perfect morning, full of happiness and laughter.

I drank a glass of water washing away the last taste of chocolate chips and walked back upstairs smiling happily that my stomach was full of my mother's homemade pancakes. I dressed with layers and stood standing still for a minute while I appreciated the fact that I was warm. I ran downstairs at full speed and fell out of the door into a pile of snow. I laid there laughing for what felt like hours and stared up at the serene sky and thought this is it...this is heaven.

I spent the whole day relishing the company of my mother while we built snowmen and attempted throwing snowballs at each other. Before they could reach either me or my mother, they collapsed in the air and fell to the ground waiting for another person to pick them up. After hours of our fun, we retired to our house where we changed into our cozy matching pajamas. I surprised my mother with a cup of hot chocolate remembering the fact that she had made me my favorite breakfast. As I grasped the outside of the mug, the hotness of it startled me, but at the same time, comfort and warmth overtook my body as I relaxed and leaned my head onto my mother's shoulder. My mother wrapped her arm around me and kissed me on the forehead as I drifted into a swift sleep.

When I awoke, it was dark outside and I smiled as I realized that there was no shining sun to wake me up. My mother had fallen asleep next to me and I rested my head back onto her shoulder for nothing could make me feel safer. For a minute I let myself just pretend as if every day could be like the one I had just lived. A life where every day all you had to worry about was having enough chocolate chips for your pancakes and the sun waking you up in the morning.

Reality quickly slapped me in the face and I realized how late it was. I got up, kissed my mom on the cheek and I closed the curtains. I made sure that they were closed all the way so that in the morning my mother wouldn't have to be bothered by the blinding sun. She could sleep in like I had the previous morning and instead I'd wake up early and cook her breakfast. I went upstairs, changed into my pajamas, opened my window, closed the curtains, and hopped back into my cozy bed with my snuggly blanket. Right before I closed my eyes, I looked at the small portion of my open curtains reminding myself that tomorrow, I would allow the bright sun to wake me up.

My own Life

By Jose Alfredo (Finalist)

Someone asked me "why I considered my life meaningful," I was speechless because there are many things that give significance to my life. I have come to understand life in both the American culture and Dominican culture, but I will first address my life from the Dominican aspect; I come from a small town in the Dominican Republic where there is no running water, electric light, and a paucity of educational opportunities. As a child, the situation in my community was drastic. Many children passed away at a young age because they did not have the medical assistance they needed and the food they consumed did not provide the required daily nutrition. The majority of people have not attended school, as the main occupation in my community has always been agriculture. My parents spent almost every day of the week cultivating the land in order to satisfy our family's basic needs. My parents' dream is that I get a good education because they do not want me to cultivate the land as my means for survival. Although, I come from a poor and honest background, I have learned I must fight for what I want in life.

I started my studies in the Dominican Republic at a small elementary school developed by the Diocese of Orlando to support the children in my village. The teachers focused on the formation of students morally, physically, spiritually, and academically. When I was younger, I did not always have a desire to study, but today both the elders and the young generation of my community look up to me for my hard work and dedication to my academic goals. Due to that hard work and dedication to my academics, the Diocese of Orlando awarded me a scholarship to study in the United States. In August 2015, I began my high school studies at Bishop Moore.

The American culture was difficult to grasp in the beginning. It was challenging because English is not my first language, and I was far from my family. I could write and read in Spanish, but I could not do it in English. I had to learn English in order to thrive at school and build relationships with other students and my teachers. I am proud to say that I am now fluent in both English and Spanish. During my time at Bishop Moore, I have become a global citizen. I associate with people from multiple nations and backgrounds. I have been well prepared academically, physically, emotionally, and spiritually at this school and have also embraced my new culture and traditions. I have demonstrated my skills and knowledge by active participation in sports, clubs, and most notably several national honor societies. I look forward to college and my future.

Aside from being a student at Bishop Moore, I have been a mentor to other students serving as an inspiration and motivator. At the end of each school year, I return home to my country to spend time with my family. During these summers, I share my knowledge with the people of my community by teaching at the elementary school and participating in spiritual events. Every time I teach them something new, the community shows their excitement and desire to acquire new knowledge which motivates me to be open to support them.

In order to acquire a good education and keep giving to the world, I desire to attend a college in which students and faculty respect the rights and ensure the welfare of everyone. I long to be part of an environment that motivates students to become responsible leaders who can find solutions to problems, support truth, and live to serve others. My goal is to get a degree in computer science and bring technology to my village. I not only dream about getting a degree, but also, desire to further develop socially, academically, and spiritually.

Until the Last Time

By Autumn Hakes (Finalist)

I have always been a soccer player. My earliest memories are out on the field. I used to think that the miniature nets to score in, and the fifteen by thirty-yard field to play on, were for babies. It did not make sense that my sister played on a real field while I was stuck with one smaller than my backyard. I thought it would be too easy to score and win. What I did not realize was that I was a baby. A four-year-old who watched professional soccer more than cartoons would have thought anything smaller than the pros would be for babies. When I was young, there was never a moment where I wasn't in the backyard with my brothers and sisters; all seven of us would run, and jump, and kick, and scream, while the bees would mosey through the periwinkle, and the tall grass would flutter in the September breeze. Of course, until we would trample it with our little callused feet. I knew it was my dream to do this forever, and I knew that I would. I had all the time in the world to make my fantasy a reality and be the best the world had ever seen. Nothing could stop my childhood dream. My parents would cheer from their camping chairs as I ran against the burning sun, on the speckled, misty, grass in the neighborhood park, elbowing my way through kids who only saw a ball. They thought that kicking the ball into the goal was the only thing that would make them happy. But that was never what made me happy. I wanted to see the game. And one day I did. Sweat poured down my face as I ran under the bright lights. Such a stark contrast from the sun. My parents were yelling from the box as I sprinted my way toward the right chalk. Faster! One, two, three, four, five- we tried to get to seven. Always seven. Seven makes them tired and give up. Seven puts us right where we want to be. Seven. I had the ball. I turned. Eighteen years of blood, sweat and tears had taught me about true happiness. I was there, and I was ready. I faced the goal. One shot and everything would be right. I ran, I ran, and I ran, but then I wasn't running. Slam. Turf in my mouth. A stab of pain in my knee. Or was it my back. My head. Pain. Sharp pain. Hard. So hard. So much pain. The flash of a camera. The flash of consciousness. The flash of the bees. And the grass. And the park. And my dream.

A Self-edited Comic

By Kyndal Bree Harrison (Finalist)

I recently auditioned for a play. It is the sort of play that requires actors to be whimsical, jaunty, and utterly optimistic. I am all of those qualities, yet I struggled to display them on the stage. I couldn't bear to let people see the pre-"self-edited" me; flailing my arms in a desperate attempt to fly, jumping from side to side like a grasshopper, or kicking my feet in a futile endeavor to resemble a mermaid. I knew I hadn't given the director anything she wanted to work with. I was dark and withdrawn when she had asked for light and uninhibited. As I left the audition, I knew I couldn't be upset with whatever casting decisions would be made. I could only wait for the cast list to come out.

Growing up, I loved to make people laugh. I could even make myself laugh. I would get up in the morning, go to the bathroom, and look into the mirror. Two dark brown, almond-shaped orbs were unblinking in their gaze. The orbs had little slices of even darker brown in them. The pupils would grow larger and I would think: Whose eyes are those? Do they belong to me? Who is me? I am me, apparently. Am I the only me in the world? In the universe? Is anyone else staring at their eyes in a fleeting attempt to truly see who they are? CLANG! I headbutted the mirror. I laughed because such thoughts shouldn't belong to people who bump noses with their own reflection. I saw myself as the joker then. The comic relief for every situation regardless of the need for one. Until one day, I didn't see the same dark brown orbs; I saw a whole face. Who is that? Why haven't I seen this before? It was my face and I saw a joke. Not the funny jokes expected at a stand-up comedy set, but a poorly executed clown trick that failed to hit the funny bone. If I was seeing my face, my joke of a face, had other people seen it before me. Even if they did, I wouldn't have it that way any longer. I didn't want people to see me as the silly little girl I used to be. The black, little girl who waved her arms for attention, rose her voice above everyone else to be heard and asked embarrassing questions about bowel movements. I decided to put myself through "self-editing".

In the reality I lived adjacent to, "self-editing" is maturing. I felt that I needed to be more forceful in my growing up. I didn't completely stop making jokes or smiling, instead, I saved my sillier, more crude jokes for my family. I changed the nature of the jokes I told my friends and peers. Unpleasantly, unprovoked fart-jokes became poignant, pointed political satire. I began reading the news and watching late night satire shows. Unbeknownst to me, I was learning and becoming aware of the busy, boundless, bumbling world I lived in. My friends didn't know about the social issues of tomorrow and when I make jokes about the need for revitalizing the one country, two systems plan, it went straight over their heads.

Until my sophomore year, these jokes went unappreciated by my peers, but I didn't mind because sometimes an adult would laugh. It was the kind of laugh that was preceded by a pregnant pause. The laugh always started with their eyes, a pair of crow's feet would appear, their eyebrows would raise in surprise, and then a sound of choked admiration would fly from their mouth and land on my hands. Before, a laugh would leave a mouth and slap my face leaving a hot mark of embarrassment. I didn't feel that when adults laughed and I reveled in the feeling of a new kind of joke. I felt as sophisticated and refined as the jokes I told. I had constructed a new persona and this was the kind of persona that didn't go well with the whimsical nature of a children's play. It was hard for me to go back to a place of deep embarrassment and channel profound happiness because I wasn't happy with who I was then. I couldn't pretend that I didn't feel absurd acting like a fairyland. I'm grounded in reality now. I know who I am, what I do and do not want, and that I don't ever want to return to who I was. I know I'm not the utterly optimistic protagonists the director desired, but I think I can do well as a pretty magnificent poetry-reciting pirate.

Panic Attack

By Elexus A Lopez (Finalist)

During this time of my life, I was all over the place. In my fourteen years of life, I never thought it would get this bad. Being upset and sad was a normal thing for me, but I never talked about it. The bottle I have inside me is full; everything wants to spill out. Once I open it to put something else inside, it's just closer and closer to breaking. The whole bottle itself is going to break glass everywhere, and it did; it broke everywhere.

Me, falling to the ground: crying, hyperventilating, the whole world spinning at 100 miles a second. Everything felt like it was falling apart, the whole earth felt like it fell with me breaking with me. Not knowing what happened or why it happened, I just broke down on the floor, the glass is everywhere.

That day was more than a panic attack it was a total meltdown. Days and nights went on and every night the skies darkened, lights flashed in the distance, cold, tears fell down my face and an empty stomach from not eating. Crying every night for weeks, my was family concerned and wanted to help but couldn't. Sitting there and crying, my sister and mom came from behind I felt their warmth, hugging and asking what they could do to help. All I heard was "mumbles". It all sounded like mumbles I couldn't hear clearly. All I could think of was why me. Another day sitting looking at lights three one flashes every second, another flash every minute, and the next flashes every hour. The next day still sitting still looking at the lights, crying and I heard footsteps then felt warmth against my back my mom tells me I need to get help because I'm not helping myself by doing this. I'm not happy and then something comes and gives a little light gives something to smile about.

I went to get help the room soft squishy couch. Sandbox soft with toy animals, rocks, and anything I could use, but I used my hands, I drew a sad and happy face because I was sad and then I had a little light. The short-haired blond women with a warming smile and a comfortable feeling trying to make me feel okay. The little light I had didn't last so long there for about two to three months and then it vanished no more light just darkness. Then I was back to square one red dots from anxiety and stress coming back and all over my arms, legs and on my eyelids, I thought to myself again why me. Sadness was back again and I never should've thought the light would be there forever. Still getting help still here getting better baby steps in all this.

Months later there's a new light that comes I don't get my hopes up never again. The light doesn't last that long but I still always have it with me waiting for it to come back. Te di un pedazo de mi corazón y mi corazón está cansado de lastimarme which means I gave you a piece of my heart and my heart is tired of getting hurt. My heart is still together but not all the way but I'm getting help and it's never something you can fix in a day but I'm getting there.

Mystery

By Mia Carrillo (Finalist)

Elisabeth Evans stood atop a building, towering over her beloved city, the night sky never looked so calming. She is seen as a hero in the eyes of citizens and to the police, a vigilante. Mystery, as they call her, only seeks revenge for the murder of her mother. Anyone with relations to the person responsible would be killed, just a quick snap of the neck. That was unless they fought back, which in this case was often. It had taken mystery years, but she finally found the man behind it all. Underneath Mayor Greer's mansion, there lies a secret cavern overlooked by the mayor's eldest son of nineteen years, Christopher.

With the speed of a cheetah, she sprints, leaving divots from every step throughout the city. Mystery arrives to the secret entrance and attempts to hack the pinned lock. How could someone so weak, so incompetent make something so advanced. She thought to herself, examining the wires cautiously wiliest flicking tools back and forth. With a long beep and intense, vibrating whirr, the black metal doors slide open. The man she was about to face had only been hiding behind his human shields his whole life, with such a frail frame Mystery expected him to be nothing without his bodyguards.

As she dashes through the seemingly endless corridor, the atmosphere grows dim until a small flash of light appears from the other side. As she approaches, she uncovers a ginormous lair with metal materials and machines scattered across the floor and walls. In the middle of it all sat 115 pounds of a tranquil slab of meat atop a computer chair, studying cryptic codes. Mystery launches five shurikens towards Christopher and everything slows. He dodges three of them. One slightly scrapes past his cheek, causing a sudden pause in movement. The other followed in suit and struck Christopher directly into his temple triggering him to fall, taking the chair down as well. His head hits the floor with a loud bang echoed throughout the cavern.

Mystery struts over to his body and lightly kicks him, "I've seen a lot of movies. Now get up." All that is left is silence making her face boil, "Get up! You son of a-" She kicks Christopher again, hard enough to tumble him over. His empty, lifeless eyes look straight ahead, the colour of his irises fade to grey. Though his eyes point forward, one might say he was looking at her. "Th-that's it," the dull and meaningless eyes staring at mystery fill her with disappointment and fear, "No, no no. That was. Too easy. He's, he's..." Her body quivers, lackluster eyes locked with one another. She starts maniacally laughing with every shortened breath.

Her legs tremble and give up, bringing her down to her knees. "Wh-what!? That was it? You were the biggest thing I feared! I spent YEARS tracking you down! You are a pathetic waste of time!" She sharply gasps from the tears trailing down her face and can't help but to think. Was it worth it? All of this just to kill this lost soul...this child. One last drop drips from Mystery's chin, tapping the floor beneath her. With her right hand, she wipes her face and slowly stands up, turns around and walks back the way she came. She exits the long corridor and stops, and looking up at the midnight sky she sheds another tear. "Please, forgive me."

Trouble in Paradise

By Grace Silva (Finalist and Honorable Mention)

It was a scorching day in the beautiful city of Madrid, Spain. My mother and I were window shopping in an outdoor mall, and all of a sudden, something felt very off. The air felt like it had changed, thicker almost. My head pounded suddenly, and my heart told me to run. I felt a nosebleed coming on. I had no time to waste, I tore through my bag and pulled out the tissues that I was lucky enough to be carrying, as I had had many awful nosebleeds in the past.

My mother was not helpful and told me to "go outside and just take care of it", so I did. I felt like screaming. I knew that what was about to happen was not going to be pretty, and my mother wanted nothing to do with helping me. I ran outside, hot from embarrassment and squatted on the stone ground with my bag. I sat behind the corner of an advertisement board, trying to hide from the world. I was beginning to run out of tissues and despite my extensive personal knowledge on how to stop a nosebleed, it wouldn't even slow down.

From behind me, I heard a woman speaking nearby and briefly glanced up, realizing she was trying to speak to me in Spanish "Estas bien? Como te puedo ayudar?", a language that I only barely understood at the time. She said to me "Estas caliente, necesita agua". I just nodded. In an instant, she pulled out a partially empty liter bottle of Luso brand water and started pouring it into her hand. She then placed her hand on the back of my neck and forehead. The water wasn't cold, but I knew she was trying to help me cool down. She did this several times before telling me she had to go and was leaving the rest of the bottle for me to drink. I thanked her quickly before she left. I was so grateful. This woman didn't know me, we didn't know each other's languages, I didn't even catch her name, but she helped me calm myself and the situation down. She was very generous, caring and kind to a random tourist on the street. That woman didn't know how much stress she relieved me from, I was and am very grateful.

Just after the first kind woman left, a pair of older women walked up to me. The bleeding had slowed a little but still was not stopping. I explained this to the pair of women that approached me who luckily, spoke English. One of the women reached into her purse and pulled out a homemade nosebleed kit. However, looking back "kit" may be an exaggeration, it was more of a plastic snack bag bursting at the seams with cotton dressing and small bottles filled with mystery substances. "I've suffered nosebleeds all my life," she said. "I finally learned to stay prepared for the worst, I'm just glad I ran into you". She took out a cotton ball and opened up a small bottle of what she later told me was oxygenated water. She soaked the large cotton ball and told me to quickly remove the tissue from my nose and look up. She then proceeded to corkscrew the drenched cotton ball into my nose.

"Ouch!" I thought. It was incredibly uncomfortable, it felt like I was drowning, but it worked. The oxygenated water hydrated my nose and held me over until we could reach a local pharmacy. I was again, so grateful to this woman for helping me in a time of need.

I was truly astonished at the kindness of people. It was a kind act of strangers who saw another person in need and didn't just walk by, but helped. I spent the rest of that trip reflecting and trying to pay it forward. Whether by picking up discarded food trays on tables, or holding the door for people behind me.

Father's Promise

By James Sam (Finalist and Honorable Mention)

It was at the start of winter,

During the snow and cold,

That the father of twins,

Had turned sixty years old.

Promising to go to the zoo,

Although he had no time,

 "On your birthdays", he says,

But he paid them no mind.

The twins constantly ask their dad,

 "Can we go to the zoo?",

And his reply always the same;

"Dad is busy but soon".

His job now becoming hectic,

With no time for leisure,

Work is more pressing than before,

His kids remain eager.

The father beginning to think,

"Maybe I should retire,

It is almost the kids' birthday,

Two words is all it would require."

One week later and now he's sick,

Seeing it as nothing,

He continues through everyday life,

With the twins still bugging.

Stress building up for the father,

It's almost winter's end,

His promise coming in two weeks,

This he can't just amend,

Day by day the father gets worse,

Telling himself it's fine,

One day he'll finally retire,

And he'll have peace of mind,

Three days until his kids' birthday,

Feeling as sick as ever,

Chest pains and sleeping at his job,

Head not getting clearer,

Two days until the twins' birthday,

The two can't sleep at night,

They ask their father one more time,

 "Zoo on our birthday, right?"

Their special day is in one day,

Today he says nothing,

Their father wakes up and just leaves,

His legs weak and dragging.

Today the father doesn't come back,

His kids believe he lied,

Their mother finds out what happened,

Turns out he had just died.

SECTION 3 – FOREVER

I'm Sorry

By Crista Ramsey (Second Place)

The baby wailed while steady, latex-gloved hands cut the cord connecting him to his mother. She loosely held him with one arm, but most of his weight settled on the hospital bed beside her. The mother's eyes were listless, with a small smile adorning her lips.

Life grinned at the small form as the crying ceased and the child slowly opened its eyes. Then another hearty wail tore from it's tiny mouth.

"Hello little one," Life cooed.

Death appeared beside Life and took in the scene. He glanced at the baby, but locked eyes with the mother. She stared back, her eyes glassy and exhausted, her thin smile dropping as she pursed her lips.

"I'm sorry," Death dropped his gaze, unable to meet the mother's eyes any longer.

Life noticed the sudden change in the atmosphere and looked across his shoulder. The look of joy and amusement immediately vanished from his face, replaced with one of horror and anger.

"You can't do this!" Life yelled, rising up and turning to face Death.

A pleading look overtook Death's face, "I-I have to. It's her time," he said despairingly.

Life shook his head, putting a hand to his temple in desperation. He looked back at the Mother, tears starting to form in his eyes. "M-Maybe I could... just-just one more time," He said, starting to walk towards her as his hand began to glow with a brilliant white light.

Death lunged at Life before his arm could reach her "No! Stop! You know you're not allowed to do that again."

Life crumpled into a heap on the glossy tiled floor, and Death fell too, holding him in a strong embrace. Life sobbed into Death's shoulder, "I just can't bear to see her go."

Death comforted him, whispering softly into Life's ear as he cried. Death knew these creations were very dear to Life, but he didn't realize the job was so close to Life's heart. Grimly, Death looked over the shoulder of the crumpled form in his arms and extended a hand toward the mother, her face as pale as the pillow case below her head. It was time to finish his job.

Life started to sit up, but Death held him back as a dark mist began to envelope his outstretched hand.

Gently, Death took the mother's hand in his, grimacing

as her eyes slowly closed. Another sob escaped from Life.

A small white dandelion fluff floated from the mother and over the shoulder of Death. Wiping his tears, Life gently pulled away to clasp the seed in his hands. It rested there for a moment before he gently blew it through the open window. It whimsically danced in the air before it was caught and carried off by the wind.

He looked back at Death, who remained on his knees, tears starting to form in his eyes. Life pulled Death into his arms, and the two faded from the sullen room.

After Life

By Ashna Vithal Divekar (Finalist)

Ba-dum, Ba-dum, Ba-dum is all I hear as the doctors started to prep me for heart surgery. The world started to fade to black as the doctors administer me the anesthetic. I woke up a while later in a warm room. The room was half red like fire and half white like light. I looked around the room to see that I was sitting in a black chair staring at the ever so flickering flame of the fireplace. As I sat in awe of my surroundings, I could hear footsteps getting closer and closer to me as my heartbeat started to beat faster and faster. I felt the presence of someone behind me, I turned around only to see no one there.

Suddenly I heard my name being called bouncing off the walls in the room. Elizabeth is all I heard as I looked around the room. I shakily replied, "whose there"... The only reply I heard back was "I am known by many names".

"What do you want," I asked.

"I am here to help you make a decision" was all I heard.

"A decision?? " I asked.

"Yes."

After that response, I was suddenly transported back in time. I saw my memories from birth to the present. I saw myself at the age of 5, falling off a tree I climbed in my backyard breaking my arm. I saw myself at age 7 finding out that my mother has cancer and watching her getting her chemo treatments only for her to get better. I saw my mother relapse again from cancer at the age of 10. The only difference this time was that cancer had reached her brain and there was no hope for her survival. Then I was suddenly thrown into the memory at the age of 11 when I was with my mother in her hospital room and how she said, "Even though I may not be with you as you grow up, I know you will grow up to be a wonderful woman. Don't let anyone tell you what to do and always be yourself. Never forget that I will always love you" as she took her last breathe and the doctors ran into the room.

I watched all my memories after the age of 12, how I pretended to be okay in front of my father, how I battled depressions with no one there for me as a teen, how I pretended to be the perfect girl to make my father happy to the memory of finding my father's body surrounded by blood with a gun next to him and a note addressed to me saying that "I am sorry, I couldn't live without her."

The last memory I saw was seeing myself getting heart surgery after getting into a car wreck. I could see the doctors yelling in the room as I started to come back to reality. "I am dying, aren't I?" I asked while crying.

"How do you know that? " asked the voice.

"I could hear the doctors yelling" I replied. Suddenly I was 2 doors form in front of me. One blue door and one red door. I walked towards the blue door after hearing my mother's voice calling out to me. Before I entered the door, I turned around one last time and I asked,

"Who are you?"

The voice replied, "What would be the fun to reveal myself" as it faded to black.

I faced my mother who brought her hand out to me and said smiling, "It`s time to come home". I took her hand as the world turned white. I was finally happy again.

The End of the Rainbow

By Willow Scott (Finalist)

It is really cold. It's usually not this cold in the small city I live in. It's the kind of cold my parents close the windows and draw their curtains to. The kind of cold that sinks into your skin no matter what you're wearing. It is also very dark. I try to blink it away but it stays heavy on my eyes. Like a night on a full moon, all the stars too far to light the sky.

I don't think my throat has ever felt as dry, my want for water increasing by the second. My brain sorts through blank memories, I can't seem to piece together the events that ended me up here. There's something faint but it's stuck at the tip of my tongue. And out of nowhere a sudden pain hits me. I breathe in so deeply it feels like my first in years. My eyes come crashing open, and I look around me. It's not like before, with the endless darkness behind my eyelids. It's bright, too bright to seem real.

Then I find the culprit of the stabbing sensation running up and down my arm. A shovel. As it continues its assault on the dirt around my arm, I find its owner with wondering eyes. My eyes meet tired ones and a face set in a grim expression. I try to speak out but all that comes is a string of rough coughs. I fight to an upright position and ignore the white spots that appear from my head feeling that it's in the sky. Despite the fuss, the shovels owner still remained undisturbed. "Where am I?" my voice hoarse as I ask a question burning in my mind.

"Welcome back, you seem like you've been down here for a while." Says my assailant in a curious voice. He stands with both hands placed on the shovels handle in front of him. He is peering at me curiously yet laid back as I search for something to say that's not entirely unintelligent.

"You come here often?" I immediately cover my face with my hand, sighing at myself. He looks at me strangely and I can tell he is contemplating burying me back up. He stays silent as he turns and walks up the ladder to the surface.

I look down at my dirt caked clothes and grimace, I really have been down here a while. "Hey! Wait for me!" I climb the ladder, trying to close the distance between a strange man I don't even know the name of.

He turns back and waits for me and then continues as I reach him. "What do I call you?" I ask as I absentmindedly brush dirt off myself and gaze over my sun soaked surroundings.

He walks with his shovel placed on his shoulder and a slight limp. He answers, "The full names' Reverie, you can call me Rev though." I nod bringing my arms to cross in front of me.

I've decided not to question my situation and just go along

with what is happening. Letting a stranger, now Rev, walk me through quiet streets until the sun starts to hide behind dark clouds. Rev guides me to a bus stop where we sit on a bench, he seems to wait for something. As a couple minutes pass, it starts to rain. I stick my tongue out and let the rain fall down my throat and wash some dirt out of my long hair. But this is short lived as the rain quickly ceases, leaving me semi-disappointed. But what replaces the rain is even more beautiful, and I feel at peace. A beautiful rainbow graces the sky, one of its ends only maybe a couple streets away.

"You aren't the only one who has always wanted to find the end of a rainbow." Rev speaks up calmly, glancing from the rainbow to me and back again. "Come, it doesn't seem too far." He gets up and starts walking down the empty street, shovel across both of his shoulders.

I stand with a mischievous smile planted on my face. "First there gets the gold!" I hurriedly shout as I pass him. I run with laughs falling out of my mouth as I watch Rev struggle with his shovel. We race like gleeful children down street after street. He never puts his shovel down and I never drop the broad smile on my face. The rainbows' end is only a street away as we finish our race with a sprint to the finish. We both crash into a patch of grass, unable to run any longer. But we had made it to the end of the rainbow.

I stand back up and turn from Rev to look for some treasure that may be laying around. "What does your name mean anyway?" I manage to ask through labored breathing.

"This," he looks around and gestures with a waving hand "all of this."

I look at him confusedly and he remains calm. "A dream." He almost whispers, but it reaches my ears loud. I close my eyes and cover my ears to try and block out the sudden noise. And everything stops.

"Stop. Stop. Stop." I repeat as I hit my head against the hard stone in front of me. My imagination stops running wild, as tears run down my face. I try to stop them with a sleeve but I fail and just let them go. I should be trying to recover from my mother's death, it's been years. But every time I kneel in front of her grave to place flowers, my mind can't help but imagine her alive. I miss her child-like nature and her nurturing ways.

And as I stand up I think about her again. How she would've disliked how I cannot let go. So I decide to hold my head high and follow my own rainbow to its end. One that is always in the sky, if I search hard enough.

Resurgan

By Victoria Shanks (Finalist)

To the elders at Berea:

Our brother Dante is dead.

He was taken the fifteenth of this month, tried a week after his arrest, and beheaded a day later. I was unable to visit him in prison, but I witnessed the execution….

{I—Dante}

TWO YEARS, nine months, and twenty-one days ago I became immortal. Call me a lunatic if you like, but it's true.

I am unkillable.

My captors can do whatever they want to my body— wound it—destroy it—but they cannot touch me, because I am more than my body. I am my soul.

And my soul? That, my friend, is untouchable.

I've harmed no-one, yet the government calls me insane, dangerous, subversive. For months I was hunted like a rabbit; my family and friends were interrogated for information on my whereabouts. I was thrown into a cell smaller than a closet, and given a sham trial. This afternoon I'm to be beaten, and publicly beheaded.

What is my crime?

I am a Christian.

{II—Elena}

"ANOTHER ONE," the girl Elena said to her friend as they watched the flogging of Dante Robinson. "Must be the fifth this year."

"At least." The friend's nose wrinkled. "It's disgusting that America still has crazies like him. How can anyone be so intolerant?"

Elena shook her hair out of her eyes. "They think everyone who's not in their cult is going to hell. Can you believe them?"

The friend laughed. "Well, in an hour there'll be one less in the world."

The guillotine is too good for them, Elena thought. The Romans had the right idea. Christians deserve to be burned alive.

{III—Dante}

WHAT DOES dying feel like, I wonder? Surely not worse than this.

I cannot walk alone to the guillotine—my legs refuse to support me after the whipping—so a guard drags me along. My back is torn, my nose probably broken. Blood is everywhere… fiery pain… and there the bladed monstrosity waits.

So many people are watching… poor lost souls! I know what it is to live without hope, like them, but what does it feel like to die without hope? They must be so afraid… Father, forgive them, they know not what they do!

I'm almost there; in two minutes I will see my Redeemer. I have nothing to fear.

By the grace of God, they can destroy my body, but they cannot touch me.

I will rise again.

…. I only pray that, when my turn comes, God will grant me the courage of Dante; who was indeed faithful unto death, and has received his crown of life.

Your brother in Christ,

Solomon

Theo

By Omid Mogasemi (Finalist)

"Not until you see the whites of their eyes, private!" The words from Theo's commanding officer rung in his head like church bells as he sprinted maniacally towards the enemy trench, feeling, but not seeing, the bodies of his fellow infantrymen dropping, almost systematically, one by one. He had no actual idea of what he would do when - no, if - he made it to the German trench - he had never really thought that far. At that point the only thought on his mind was making it to the other side, so he stuck his head down between the barrage of bullets and let his M97 drag across the dirt as he carried it in his right hand.

Then, suddenly, there was a stinging feeling in Theo's right shoulder. He knew damn well what it was but he kept going, being sure to not stop to even think or risk a dishonorable discharge. So he continued to sprint, focusing on the rhythm of his feet against the blood-stained dirt. But as his legs pounded forwards and the ring of mortar rounds being volleyed overhead pierced his ears, everything started to become a haze. The ground beneath him now seemed miles away, as if his ankles were clouded in a morning fog, and the chilling screams of men dying around him began to fade. He could feel himself slowing down, and his partner behind him giving him a shove to keep going. But despite mustering every ounce of strength in his body, Theo could not. Step by step he slowed down, until, for a brief moment, the world around him grew eerily quiet, like a cemetery in the dead of night.

Then, suddenly, Theo found himself at the doors of his town's local restaurant, the winds of a cool, quiet April night nipping at his ears as he ducked inside. That night was supposed to be the celebration of his accomplishments in grade school, and his recent graduation. Theo had never been much like his classmates in school - he chose to focus on academics instead of partying or making friends, and it showed when he was announced to be at the top of his class at the end of his final year. As Theo entered the restaurant, he immediately spotted his family in the dimly lit back corner, with concerned looks on their faces. Walking with long, quick strides to their table, Theo knew what the problem was before he even got there. He had been drafted.

But right as Theo entered his final long stride as he approached their table he was suddenly fourteen, his legs transformed into a long sprint towards a lake as the pitch of his classmate's shrieks inundated his ears, causing him to lose all sense of the green forest that surrounded him. He dove headfirst into the lake, not stopping even to remove his clothes, and grabbed her by the hand, fighting desperately against her kicks to stay above water. He dragged her as hard as he could, paddling against the ice cold January water that threatened to freeze his limbs at any moment. After nearly ten minutes of this seemingly hopeless struggle, Theo reached the water's end and stumbled out of the lake with the girl's icy-cold hand still gripping for life onto his before he finally broke off and fell face first out onto the grass, exhausted.

Theo was then eleven, lying face down in his bed. His cheeks were puffy and his eyes red, as his father had delivered the so-dreaded speech to Theo that his mother had not made it, and that her funeral was to be next Monday. Theo could barely contain himself, as tears continued to stream down his cheeks as his body underwent uncontrollable shuddering. The woman who had raised him, and been there every day when his father went off to the factory to play games with him, to take him to the park, to teach him how to cook, was not as invincible as she once seemed. Theo flailed his arms wildly, banging his pillow with all his might as if he wanted to teach it a lesson for what had happened to his mother.

But all of a sudden Theo found himself nine, shaking his arms in the air in an excited frenzy as his father walked through the door, his first week's salary in hand and a stuffed bear in the other. His father, the hardest working man he knew, had finally found a job after nearly two years of unemployment, and now he walked through the door, stained in grease, his face blackened by the soot from the line and his hands calloused and bruised. But Theo couldn't care less, and he ran excitedly up to his dad, squeezing him around his waist as the dirt jumped onto his clothes.

Then, as if he had never left, Theo was back in the heat of battle, struggling again to see his ever-slowing legs. But no matter how much he tried he couldn't, and unsure of where his feet were Theo soon tripped and fell to the ground, too sluggish to even attempt to catch his own fall as his face planted itself in the dirt, the taste of blood now on his tongue. And then, in what was seemingly no less than a second, Theo was no longer Theo. He now had been stripped of his identity, of everything unique and ordinary about him, and he became one, just one of sixteen million, an indistinguishable statistic in the sea of those who now looked just like him. He was dead.

Interview with Emanuel Quena

By Jada Broome (Finalist)

EMANUEL Quena. Everything you know and love is because of him. All those cool trips you took in middle school. Actual footage of World War II that you got yourself for a documentary (I'm looking at you, Errol Morris). That's who I'm talking to today. His heels clack on the ground of the World Cafe, where we are meeting to discuss his newfound success. Quena is just five feet tall and wears high heeled boots to look taller. His hair is salt and pepper. He seems so outstandingly average for the man who changed the world.

As he settles down, I introduce myself. "Jedidiah Morgan," I say, extending my hand. "But you can call me Jed. And might I add-- It's such a pleasure to meet you. Are you ready to start?"

He nods, and we both receive steaming cups of coffee (his vegan, mine not), which we sip throughout the interview.

Me: So, what was your childhood like?

Quena: My parents weren't rich, but they weren't poor. We couldn't afford many newer books, but I was basically always surrounded by history books. My mother volunteered at the museum in our town. Sometimes I went with her. Oh--this is also important to the story--my mother is white. We often visited England, where her family is from, and there, I found out about Doctor Who. It was one of my favorite shows at the time. The concept of the future and the past drew me in and were the foundations of some of my fondest childhood memories.

Me: Okay, so time travel has obviously always been a really important idea to you; but what moved it from childhood fantasy to a real-world application?

Quena: It was one day when I was in university, I was thinking, y'know, the past already happened. It's established. It's fixed. Shouldn't we be able to go back to it? It's kind of like--okay, here's what went through my mind--the Great Wall of China. It's fixed. Once it was built, it would be here forever, and therefore we can go and see it. Feel it. Experience it. So to me, time was like that. Er, the past, more specifically. It already happened. An event was already built.

And what about the 'time machine'?

Quena: Well, just like how we have to take a plane to get from the States to China, I figured we needed some way to get back in time. It sounds silly, saying it out loud because of course, we can't just whisk ourselves back in time without a way to get there. But that was essentially my reasoning.

Me: What were some of your experiments to test your theory?

Quena: Well, light, for one, since the light we see from stars comes to us from deep in the past. I did a couple of light experiments, but those didn't really prove my point. So I did a few more...dangerous experiments. Built a prototype time machine and put my pet rat in it. That was the last time I saw him. Who knows? Maybe he's stuck in the fifteenth century. I doubt it, though, since my machine stayed right where it was with smoke coming from the sides.

Me: What led up to the most successful version?

Quena: It was on one of many late nights in December of 2002. I placed a ring--I was done with doing live experiments--inside the device. I had a remote control that I used and a small camera I placed on the outside of the machine. I was so close to giving up as I pressed the button. I watched on my old college student TV screen as the machine zoomed out of perspective and I saw...well, you know if you've ridden the Train. It was amazing...everything blinked into view as 1865. I sent the machine back...the ring was intact. You wouldn't believe my elation. After that, I presented it to the National Science Board. They funded it and got me a team of engineers who worked on larger prototypes.

Me: What was the most difficult part of managing the Trains?

Quena: I think getting them widespread. Y'know...getting some of my engineers to go to different time periods and spread around, "Hey, hundreds," no, "Thousands of years in the future people are going to figure out how to come back here. It's going to be a great tourist destination." We've done a great deal of history changing, also. Someone takes a selfie with Alexander Graham Bell and he's slacked off on making the telephone since we have cooler ones now. People working on the first railroad seeing this train just appear out of nowhere that's almost 200 years more advanced. We had to let all sorts of people know that our busiest days are Saturdays and Fridays and that newlyweds would crash their sockhop, or that a crowd of Christians and Jews might show up a little ways away while Moses is getting the Ten Commandments. Just telling these people that are so far behind modern technology that 21st-century humans will show up is so difficult. Telling them to do everything like normal. Especially when that one kid wants to go down and yell at the Hebrews, "DON'T BUILD THE GOLDEN CALF", and the train operator has to go back before then just to erase it.

Me: Elaborate on the whole Moses situation...

Quena: Heh, I'd rather not. Just know that the early days of the Train were pretty messy and rules got wayyyy stricter over time.

I tell Quena about how when the Train first came to our area when I was a nineteen year old, washed out, failing college student, it filled me with hope and convinced me I could follow my dream of being a journalist. "That's amazing," he says with a laugh. "I never knew I would impact so many people with my dumb old idea."

History speaks for itself--Quena's invention was anything but dumb. It convinced many children--especially minority children--that they could do anything. That any outlandish dream could come true.

Wobbly

By Iris Wright (Finalist)

"I attract wobbly chairs," Madeleine's voice reached Burk's metallic ears just after her frown reached his multi-faceted eyes. They triggered a desire to be useful, but he had not downloaded the software for repairing chairs; it took almost 12 hours to upload, and he rarely made time for learning skills he wasn't sure he would use. He was also not designed to calculate complex probabilities, so he had no background in the forces that pulled inadequate chairs into the paths of beautiful women.

He felt completely wrong for this gorgeous human sitting before him. What could he offer her that another man— a real man—couldn't provide? He glanced around his mental map of the patio without moving his eyes. The only other droids he spotted were waiters. Even they had more useful skills that be had. They could fix this chair. Better yet, they could determine how wobbly a chair was before Madeleine or anyone else sat in it, providing a life for her that was free from all wobbly chairs.

Leading up to Madeleine's chair statement, Burk's wires had been glowing with anxiety. When he stepped through the restaurant's glass door from the sidewalks on the cleaner side of the city, he was concerned first with the stares he might receive from diners and second with if he had arrived too early and risked appearing too eager. He glanced around, but no one had looked up to inspect his lit eyes.

The host was not a droid. The other droids in Burk's side of the city might call him a "flesh," but Burk never felt comfortable with the term. The non-droid host led Burk to his date, Madeleine, who was already seated. She'd chosen a wire chair outdoors. The blue paving on the patio reflected cool light onto her soft features.

The host handed Burk a menu and departed. Burk sat down, but the motion felt interminable, like he was lowering himself to the seat in slow motion. Madeleine acknowledged his presence with her eyes, and he felt a surge of paranoia that she was watching his movements for robotic tendencies.

She was prettier than her dating profile picture. She had a round face and a posture that implied she was proud of her large figure. Her hair sat on her head in feathery wisps, and her eyes glimmered beneath a cloud of fatigue. Burk hadn't downloaded many programs, but he had learned to navigate the internet better than even most droids. Finding Madeleine had been a victory. Seeing her in person was a test in self-confidence and social skills that he feared would malfunction.

"It's great to meet you in person." Relief washed over him when he heard his artificial voice box function smoothly.

"Yes, you too," she seemed to attempt a smile that she was too tired to accomplish.

It was a Friday night, so Burk assumed she was exhausted from the work week. He tried to imagine working as a surgeon, but his knowledge of the human body was limited, so his imagination only produced a picture of his own work. He was a humanoid engineer. He operated on droids, replaced parts, repaired shorted circuits, installed larger memory banks in the droids who could afford them.

His knowledge of the human body was about as extensive as his knowledge of dating. Burk had never been on a date before tonight. Once in middle school he had asked a girl to the school dance. His middle school crush's exact words, coded into Burk's memory banks, were: "Ew! You're a robot. No one wants to go to the dance with you."

His droid friends advised him to date other droids. While tying his tie in the mirror earlier that night, his roommate had said, "Hey, man, don't worry if this doesn't work out tonight. I can hook you up with that girl from my work. She's the cutest droid. Trust me on this one."

His preference for human girls had nothing to do with a lack of trust in his friends. It wasn't due to any fault he found in girls made of metal and wires, either. He was comfortable with droid girls, but rarely as more than friends. When it came to attraction, to the relationship he envisioned for his future self, it was always with a human.

Madeleine's dating profile said she liked droids— actually, according to Burk's memory banks, it said, "Open- minded surgeon, seeking relationship with male, open to dating robots." Though Burk preferred "droid" to "robot," he took a chance.

When their waiter showed up, he was also not a droid, and his hair was more attractive than Burk's wig. He remembered their drink orders without writing them down, which Burk noted because it made him feel his memory skills were mundane. The drink menu had an uncommonly wide selection of droid-friendly options, which made Burk feel slightly less uncomfortable but also slightly less unique.

When the waiter left, Burk organized the overlapping functions buzzing around his metal skull to attempt conversation. "Have you been to this restaurant before?"

"Yes, it's one of my favorites," Madeleine said. "They have the best salads here."

"I like the décor." He hoped he sounded polite without sounding boring.

"My only complaint is this chair," she shifted her weight, and the chair tipped, lifting one of its metal legs off the ground. Then she said, as if disappointed with the universe, "I attract wobbly chairs."

His hard-drive whirred with words he could say. He registered the feelings of helplessness, inadequacy, and an inability to fit in with his surroundings. Madeleine tipped her chair back to its position, and for a split second her movement fit Burk's schema for falling. He realized his solution. Looking into Madeleine's eyes, he stood. His own chair pushed back as he rose. Madeleine's head tipped upward to hold his gaze.

"Here," he charged his voice with as much confidence as he wished he had. "You can have my chair."

The Enlightenment

By Chloe Cattaneo (Finalist)

The darkness of the concert hall reminded Mila of her bathroom.

The rest of the family had known not to intrude during Mila's hour of solitude. Once a week, lights off, fully dressed, she lay in water skinned with lavender oil, hot enough to melt her to the bone. She would watch the air gather itself before her, then disperse at the last moment before it became substance. With the shades drawn it was dark enough to do this.

And since Mila had been born unable to hear, it was always silent enough.

Once the pain from the water's heat dulled and her sleeve stopped tricking her into believing it was a spider, Mila could feel her body easing away from her. Into nothingness. Toes first. The eyes, the hair, always last.

Her hours of solitude gave Mila's life the weight, the layers it so desperately craved. Behind every petty argument, every schoolyard tantrum and failed quiz grade, there was the gentle reminder of being nothingness and everythingness. Being a dot, collecting and recollecting itself, never tangible, never qualifiable, yet irreplaceable.

Since Mila had never undergone speech therapy and wasn't much of a writer, she had never quite managed to convey the meaning of her hour of solitude to anyone. For her family it just reinforced their notions of her peculiarity. A gray-eyed, rail-thin deaf girl who organized pebbles in rows at the corner of the schoolyard and carried a playing card in her pocket, Mila's family ceased their struggles to understand her before they even began them.

Mila didn't mind. She lived for the solace of her hour when she could choose, rather than be forced, to feel that she was nothing. She stuck to the darker half of the sidewalks on her way home, hopping from shadow to shadow, a gloomy hopscotch. Never did she wonder what words were framed by the ever-moving lips of passerby, her teachers, parents, classmates. She did not need to know.

At seventeen, Mila found herself mistaken for a soccer ball. Having tripped on her way across the soccer field, unaware that she was directly in the path of a two hundred pound boy in soccer cleats, she was kicked forcefully and directly in the head.

Suddenly, the air had a fullness, a substance to it. The dots she had watched collecting in the dark of her bath had collided- splitting her world in two. Feeling as if gravity had been inverted, Mila didn't have the capacity even to wonder as that was drowned out by the clashing of her surroundings-echoes blooming from her periphery and entering her ears, astonishingly painful, unrelenting. Like color, conceptualized, burning the insides of her ears and brain with their intensity and drama. Mila felt woozy and sick. Involuntarily, she lifted her hands to shield her eyes, to wish for nothingness.

The doctors, her parents, pronounced it a miracle. Mila was more hesitant. A week after her hearing was restored, Mila finally ventured a walk outside- wearing headphones. She went to the corner and back. Her footsteps scared her.

Over the next few months, Mila began to risk longer walks. Earmuffs, instead of her headphones. Her mother's laugh- how it trilled out of her, rushing and sweet, like the water under a pump- left soft rings in Mila's head and brought tears to her eyes. She would stand at the kitchen counter and pour cups of water out into empty cups, then pour them back again, loving the thrill it sent up her spine. Muzac made her arms tingle. The tap of a pencil on the edge of a desk, a heavy exhale, the scrape of a butterknife on toast, made her smile.

By the time a year had gone by, Mila's hours of solitude gave way to lukewarm, rushed showers. She stood at busy intersections, savoring the clamor of crosstown traffic, took trains into the city to hear street vendors shout, children wail, pub crawls migrate from bar to bar. For the girl floating in the tub she felt only pity, a kind of sad, sickly fondness for her past ignorance.

Her favorite was concert halls. In clicking high heeled shoes and rustling dresses, Mila sat as close to the front row as her budget would allow. As soon as the conductor lifted his hand, her body strained forwards, her blood hot, face flushed, hands trembling. Then the orchestra would begin to play and she would sob, shoulders shaking against her seat, sure that she had divined the secret to beauty, to passion, to grandeur, the reason to murder a lover, drown oneself in a white dress, open your mouth and fling your arms wide to catch the rainfall. She had peeled back every layer, down to the soft, pulsating center of what it meant to be alive.

That night in her city hotel room, Mila felt a pervasive melancholy that did not let her eat, did not let her sleep. At half past one she rose from bed and went to the bathroom, leaving the lights off and her pajamas on.

Before her eyes, the air did not collect and rearrange itself. Her body did not erase. It lay there, like a dead thing in a tub. Mila felt a uselessness- a longing. For the cautious way she had moved through shadows, for the conscious effort to remember the feeling of nothingness- a feeling she could no longer recall- and incorporate it into her thoughts, actions, wonderings. She tried to conjure the silence that had once been the whole of her reality. Found she could not.

Mila climbed out of the tub. The water was far too hot, and was hurting her.

Weapon N-074

By Lia Ahmed-Zaid (Finalist)

You are a weapon, and weapons don't weep. That's what they tell us at the Facility. It's simple logic. There's no use in crying. It's a waste of energy, and displays weakness. The cadets are supposed to be stoic, so they must not cry.

I don't mind the rule. There's not much for me to cry about anyways. You get used to the procedures after a while, and the assignments don't bother me if I don't think too hard about them. They're just tasks to complete, boxes that need to be checked off. I have no reason to complain. They provide us with everything we need here at the Facility, and I enjoy the structure and rigidity of the routine. There's no uncertainty or chaos in the PSYSOC Program. Everyone knows what to do and when to do it. Conflicts are rare, and when an accident does occur, the board ensures that it's taken care of quickly and discreetly. Each rotation of the day is calculated precisely, ensuring optimal efficiency.

I've been a SOC cadet for four years. All cadets are recruited at age eight, once the examination is administered and results are analyzed. Those scoring high in tactical capacity and low in emotional capacity are prime targets for the PSYSOC Program. If the candidate is selected to become part of the force, they are involuntarily enrolled in the Program. It's a high honor, as cadet is a highly respected position. Once you're in the Program, they set your schedule and training regimes, as well as any assignments that may arise.

My team is heading out for an assignment now. The briefing agent labeled it as another common disruption. The insurgents are becoming more restless, and their camps are increasingly difficult to locate.

The truck stops. We must have arrived. The captain of my team, a PSY cadet in her fifteenth year, directs us to gather our equipment and file into formation. We move swiftly and silently through the forest. Suddenly, the captain motions for us to stop at the edge of the brush surrounding the rebel camp. We separate, branching out to surround the target. I wait patiently in position. The only sound I hear is my breathing. My heartbeat is normal. Four years of missions have numbed any anxieties or panic. I have one goal. I will complete that goal.

My communicator lights up; that's the signal for those of us on offense. I detach my thoughts from the moment, and let my body do the rest. Everything becomes a blur. Targets taken out, threats eliminated, it's all nothing new. My mind is focused on the task at hand, nothing else.

Except her. A woman, shaking, her hiding place exposed. Something about the way she reaches out for her child catches my attention. Some quality of desperation in her cries jolts me awake. I've hesitated, and lost my target. Something is tight in my chest. It must be frustration. I need to work quickly now, or I'll be in trouble with the captain.

My team works fast, and within minutes we're back on the van. I sit in silence on the trip back. Thoughts are circling around in my head, a jumbled catastrophe. I don't like it.

I wake up in the middle of the night in a cold sweat. I had a dream. It was a vision of a woman, crying out, trying desperately to grasp at her child. I know this woman, this moment. I put my head in my hands, trying to remember. This wasn't a vision, but a memory, one deeply repressed and forgotten. I was the child, and the woman was my mother. This was the day I was taken to the Facility and enrolled in the PSYSOC Program. My mother didn't understand how much of an honor this was. She couldn't see that I would be going to serve my country that I would protect the government. She didn't want me to go. I remember her crying, telling the officials that there must have been a mistake, that I was a good girl, that I didn't deserve this. That image of my mother's tear-stained face, hands straining to catch something perpetually beyond her reach, was burned into my mind.

There it is again, that tightness in my chest. It's uncomfortable, and it makes it hard to breath. There's a hot, itchy sensation behind my eyes, one I've never experienced before. My vision is blurring, my head is cloudy, and my eyes ache. I reach up to rub them. They're wet.

Tears.

I'm crying. It's sloppy and shameful, but tears keep coming. I let the tears fall, and in the morning I tell no one.

I've never had these kinds of feelings before. Is something wrong with me? I'm not physically injured, but I feel great pain. I don't understand it. I can't stop thinking about my mother. I haven't seen her in four years. What happened to her after I was taken away? Does she cry over me? What is she doing now? Is she even alive?

I think I miss her.

Time passes. The rebel force is getting stronger and larger, and the board seems nervous. My team is receiving more frequent assignments, with more targets to eliminate. I'm afraid to continue as an offensive agent, worried I'll run into another distraction like that rebel woman. I ask the captain to switch me to defense, and she's suspicious, but she complies. I have a feeling I should keep what happened a secret. There's no doubt that I would be punished.

So I push my feelings deep down inside myself, and try to forget. Every once in a while, I have the dream again. It's different now. The scene is blurry, and the sound is muted. Each time, it becomes more and more distorted. The only thing that remains is the hot itchy sensation, but I shed no tears. I am a weapon, and weapons do not weep.

Xenon's Unending Turbulence: The Beginning

By Alexandra Clark (Finalist)

Vast, cold, and infinite, like a growing shadow, it's easy to be lost in the murky depths of space. Deep in desolate space, a lonely ship wanders for a new home, named in dirtied and worn letters as "Saint GENES1S." In it are the people of Xena, a kind and native people, who loved their home, and were born one with the earth of it, are now fleeting against time after their home world perished and burned at the hands of deadly conquerors. Amongst them is Xenon, as much a child of Xena as anyone else, yet forever an outsider is alone looking out from their now metallic home. He glances back at his family and few friends, yet finds himself numb, and lost. Today was just like any other day, in fact, it was impossible to detect one day from another, as there was no moon, sun, or familial stars for one to devote to. Yet still, it was just another mundane day in surviving. Xenon turned away from the small smudged window to go to the personal care sector, where usually busy, he didn't see a soul in sight. He didn't think much to himself, thinking perhaps there's just nobody loitering in the sector common hall. He continued to the hygiene branch, full of showers, sinks, and public baths. Once again, nobody, not even a whisper or trace of someone. Xenon preferred being alone anyways, and undressed out of his thin suit.

After a long warm shower, Xenon simply dressed, and went to the sinks. He ran the cold water over his hands, then cupping in, and oddly enough, staring at his small, rippling reflection. "Damn you." Slashing the cold water on his face, Xenon felt ready to deal with today. The door to the showering and bathing hall swung open, and Xenon in a panic quickly put on his gloves and just as he was about to leave, Xenon felt a huge force shake the whole room. On the floor, he looked to see who opened the door, and realized they had a weapon, a heavily advanced gun of some sort, and they didn't look alike to any of his people. Just as they were about to glance towards his direction, Xenon ran towards the public baths which were individually separated by short porcelain walls. Crouched in the hot bath, Xenon with panic in his breath awaited for the stranger to leave. After what felt like eternity, he heard the footsteps slowly fade away, and the door squeaked open, and slammed shut. Xenon glanced past the wall with nervous eyes, and close to the floor, looked out in the common area, and with no danger in sight, sighed with relief. His moment of peace was over just as soon as it started, "where's my family?" Xenon ran towards the door, and just as he reached for the handle, he felt a second, more intense power shake the vessel with vigor, and a horrible, numbing, ringing in his ears, and a more horrible fear for everyone else. He staggered towards the door, and opened it into a hell hotter than one can imagine.

Pain, death, and fire now filled the once formidable and cold ship. Xenon was losing everything familiar, everything he loved before his eyes. He ran towards where he last saw his parents, near the window. As he arrived at the small window, he looked in panic, not his mother, father, or friends in sight. He glanced at the window, and saw his once empty view now was filled with a deadly predator. Another ship, covered with stolen scrap and metal from its victims seemingly was now attached to their vessel. Hyperventilating on smoke choked air was throwing Xenon into full on panic. "Over there! There's another one!" Xenon turned and saw a stranger, alike to the first one, but different. Xenon froze at first, and hesitated to run, but after seeing the stranger get ready to aim, he ran. Xenon ran for his life, tripping over the occasional dead, seeing his people fade away as they were hauled and pushed into a foreign light, he looked all over for anyone to save as he ran. There was nobody left but the dead. Xenon ran into the food sector, where he knew he could hide among the aisles and many vending stands. Desolate and destroyed. There was no fire, but it was obvious that whoever was there struggled, and was either dead, or now hostage. Xenon hid behind one of the vending stands and caught his breath. He walked around to each area of the ship, now with a pipe he found among the rubble, and knew he was the only one of his people left on the vessel. With a painful sorrow, he wailed over and over "Hello?! Anyone?! Is anyone here, is anybody hurt?!." No answer. Minutes passed and became hours, and the flames died away, yet the damage inflicted to the ship was eating away to it, and quickly. Air was still leaking away, and fast, and Xenon, slowly becoming more and more disorientated knew he had to flee his home once again.

Xenon got on the only undamaged escape pods,

buckled up, and started it up. With little knowledge on how to work on, he managed to get off the dying vessel, and was now confronted with the challenge of finding a nearby planet or station that could be of any help. Hours passed, and Xenon was enveloped by a horrible headache, and now again, the ringing. Red flashing everywhere, beeping and buzzing. Xenon judged the pod wrong, the fuel container was damaged, and leaking. Xenon wasn't scared, just tired, and faced only two options, definite death, or traveling at hyperspeed to either help, or death. He chose possible death. The stars smeared across the glass, and in an instant, the vessel crashed into trees and earth. Disorientated and bleeding, Xenon got out and saw a heavenly light afar reading, "EDDY'S BAR."

Why I'm The Way I Am

By Peter Pham (Finalist)

Sundays had always been my favorite day of the week, as they were reserved for hours of skating, relaxing, and spending time with family. With my brother upstairs (most likely sleeping in), we decided to start breakfast without him. The room filled with our laughter as my sister and mother fire back-to-back stories to each other, making the conversion feel like a heated basketball game with each person trying to one-up the other with a better story.

The laughter suddenly stopped when we all heard a thud coming from upstairs. My mother insisted that we checked on it even after I had ensured her that it must've been my brother in the restroom, accidentally slamming the toilet seat down as he was using it. She ignored me and hastily proceeded upstairs to check on him. As my sister continued to recite her stories, it was quickly interrupted by my mother's scream. She had yelled out my brother's name, prompting me to run into our shared room. My mother was lying next to my brother's stiff body, crying, pain running throughout her entire vocal cords. The walls looked like a Pollock painting, with our green walls now accented by the contrasting red blood splatters. His head was half gone and his brain was visible. A gun laid mingled between his fingertips, the barrel staring at me like an attentive cadet to his superior.

Throughout the entire grieving process, I was told over and over again, "You're a man, don't cry. Be strong for your family." Coming from a background of many macho figures of authority, it was always obvious to me, even as a young child, that crying was something only girls did. With every tear that has ever slipped from my eyes, I'm reminded of the defining qualities of a man, and that crying was not one of them. But I felt conflicted with the reserved, emotionless personality I naturally have with the feelings of depression that were consuming me. I was taught to never speak my thoughts, subsequently making it difficult for me to find a way to relieve the emotions that I felt.

It was with the help of my sister that I was able to overcome these emotions. We would talk and cry to each other, remembering our brother and all the happy moments we had with him. I told her about my grief, and how it was affecting my life. I was unable to sleep at night, having visions of my brother ingrained permanently in head. I also struggled in the last months of school. I told her how school felt longer, lectures become less important, and my work ethic became nonexistent.

Throughout this experience, by simply speaking to my sister and trading my private personality for a personality that left me feeling vulnerable, I was able to cope with the pain. Having someone there to listen to what I had to say not only gave me the comfort to speak of my brother's death, but also of the other issues that I was dealing with: insecurities, self-worth, and identity. On an even grander scale, this experience shaped who I am. Prior to this, I was always to myself, never getting personal with anybody around me (even my closest friends). I gained the courage to confront the depression and grief that I was feeling, and admitted to myself that I needed help. I knew that I had to forget what everyone had told me in the past about "being a man" and trust the people around me that truly cared about my well-being. Learning to speak my mind and overcoming the fears of expressing my thoughts, I was able to overcome my emotions and feel comfortable with communicating my pain to the people around me.

Grass

By Anna (Finalist)

Every step I take, I feel the damp grass below my feet. I smell the fresh air flowing around me, that wonderful smell of dried leaves, of rain, of grass. I hope this day lasts forever, stays with me wherever I go. All the colors of the sky start to blur together and now I can't feel the grass. I know it's there, I just can't feel it. It doesn't scare me though, I'm used to this blind feeling. The feeling that runs through my veins every day, like a spark running on a wire. That feeling gets stronger every day.

Eventually, I fall to my knees, unable to stand anymore. I don't remember when I start laughing, I just know I do, I hear it. A faint echo in my ears. I run my hands along the soft grass unconsciously. It follows the path of my painted hand, then goes back to its swaying position. I can hear the grass move now, its small movement sounds like a crashing wave on a rocky beach. I smile slightly, as I can't do much in this dazed state. I like this feeling.

It's gotten a little dark since I've been out here, though the sun hasn't moved at all. I can hear the leaves falling, and the birds singing, but I can't see any of them. My wrists have started to feel numb, and my hands have begun to shake. I can hear a faint voice in my head telling me to go back inside, but I block it out. I wanted to be outside, with the beautifully painted grass.

The numbness continues to flow through my body, luring me into a wonderful dark and sweet void. Little droplets of water run down my body, I can't tell if it's rain or sweat anymore. My head feels heavy, so I lay down. The cold grass rubs my nose, it tickles. I can't see the grass anymore, but the picture is burned in my thoughts.

The spot of red paint on the black grass is getting larger. Its crimson color fills my mind, as my last seconds of consciousness come to their end. All I can think about is the wonderful feeling of finally letting go, ending my life in the most beautiful spot in the world. In the grass.

I have one thought before I finally fall under deaths spell:

Grass will be beautiful, no matter what color it is painted.

Forever Young

By Ashlyn Athey (Finalist)

"Darling, you look absolutely marvelous," cried his sister, Angelica, with delight as she pinned a crimson red rose to the pocket of his tweed suit.

"Well, what can I say? It's what the clothing machine picked out for the celebration," he flashed a grin at her as he attempted to squeeze past the colorful guests crowding the hardwood foyer as music floated in the background.

The aromatic smells of lemon pepper chicken roasting in the automatic oven wafted his way. The dazzling dining room beckoned to the famished guest while he took in the lively atmosphere dancing around him through steel blue eyes.

"Angelica, is this new?"

The pale, slender fingers were fiddling with a simple gadget the size of his thumb lying on the entrance table.

"Oh, I haven't told you? Why, it's the Teleporter 300 Ronaldo helped invent. He brought it for the party tonight and thought we could have fun teleporting each other anywhere in the world, or at least that's what he said," she giggled through cherry lips like a schoolgirl.

"Ah, sport, it's good to see you!"

A high-pitched voice barely reached his sensitive ears as a portly man sauntered over with a hand-rolled Cuban cigar languidly drooping out of his thick lips to shake the sinewy hand still grasping the gizmo.

"So you've met my little contraption," the unshaven face forced a chuckle as the chubby fingers snatched it away from his brother-in-law with such speed the latter didn't even know was possible.

"If you'll excuse me the technology is recently new, and I'd like to keep it that way. Nothing personal, old chap. Just a little habit of mine."

The ferret-like eyes squinted under the gold-rimmed round spectacles barely supported on a fresh, childlike face as his brother-in-law returned the uncomfortable gaze coolly back.

"Well, what do you two say to dinner?" Angelica eagerly suggested as she herded the crowd of chattering guests into the dining room where the elm table, covered with a pearly white tablecloth, was rapidly set by robotic housemaids for a splendid three-course dinner.

"Champagne, sir?" an automated voice croaked at Angelica's brother as the steel tentacles whipped up his glass and carefully poured a bubbly, amber substance into it.

"You'll like it, sport. It's to get us all cheery for Carmen's first birthday," Ronaldo attempted to squeak over the noise of the company as he leaned over to point to his bright-eyed daughter, clapping her tiny hands in a self-adjustable highchair.

He nodded with a weak smile at Ronaldo's remark, impatiently eyeing the coconut shrimp appetizer the robotic housemaid was now bringing around the endless table when Angelica's smooth voice piped up.

"This is our third child, isn't it dear? I can't seem to keep track of them now," she sighed.

"Yep. That's how we stay forever young, isn't it old sport?"

Waves of nausea suddenly overtook his trembling form as the bright kitchen lights blurred out of view. He dashed to the nearest restroom, and after ripping off his tweed blazer, sat lifelessly on the cream-colored bathroom tile.

He knew exactly what would happen to Carmen. This was his third time visiting his sister's spacious mansion for his nieces' birthday parties, and each time he endured it in an almost ritual-like manner with a foolproof smile. The doctors would pay their visit towards the end of the celebration. The doctors with those beady eyes constantly shifting would seize the innocent child and plod back to that metallic van as if she were nothing more than an ordinary package. Then they would haul her off to the whitewashed, stucco building they coined "the hospital," in which the child's fresh DNA would be transplanted into her parents. Their aging genetic material just wouldn't do for modern society today. The adults desperately needed to remain youthful, and, in their vain lust, they hastily stepped on the toes of youngsters who never had a fair chance at life. All of this he knew, and he knew all too well.

A sharp rattle at the restroom door jolted his mind back down to reality as he wearily placed the tweed blazer back onto his heavy laden shoulders and staggered over to turn the brass knob.

"Goodness man, don't you know there's a line out here," scratched a voice that belonged to a short-haired blonde woman.

The steel blue eyes were already firmly set, and, taking little notice of her, he strode back into the boisterous dining room, where he gingerly sat down in the seat next to Ronaldo.

"You missed a most wonderful dessert, old chap. The maid served yellow birthday cake. Imagine that—"

A robotic maid clumsily tripped, spilling an entire bottle of champagne all over Ronaldo's new tuxedo. In his horror, the pudgy man sprung from his seat and began to scold the machine. Meanwhile, his brother-in-law discreetly slipped his hand under the tablecloth to reach the Teleporter 300 that had fallen onto the hardwood floor from within the velvet lining of Ronaldo's pocket.

Mentally screaming Carmen's name, he pressed the maroon red button on the side of the gadget he had discovered earlier, and instantly found himself lying senseless on the frigid tiled kitchen floor in his desolate apartment. Frantically, he began desperately tearing through all the rooms in the absolute dark, attempting to discover his one-year-old niece peacefully resting somewhere. He dashed into the bedroom with yesterday's yellowed undershirt strewn upon the carpet, the living room with spaghetti still stubbornly stuck to the blue plastic plate, and then he found–

He woke up shrieking in sweat-drenched checkered bed sheets, running a sweaty palm through his unkempt charcoal hair as he attempted to subside the dizzying headache that gripped his mind when a nasally, familiar voice echoed from a desolate corner of his bedroom.

"Hello, sport. I'm missing a little gizmo of mine."

As a gunshot rang out, the crimson red rose fluttered out of his tweed suit.

The Day It All Changed

By Virginia Hughes (Finalist)

"Sometimes our lives have to be completely shaken up, changed, and rearranged to relocate us to the place we're meant to be."- unknown. This quote represents what happened to me just this year. It all started when my great grandpa went to the hospital. He was 98 years old at the time. He was quite active for his age. He could walk perfectly and do so many things most 98-year-old men can't do. He even rode a roller coaster with me when he was 92! I call my great grandpa, Peepaw. He owns 70 acres of fields where he grows crops to sell in the stores. He worked with an assistant to grow crops ever since his wife passed away a couple of years before. He would go to his pasture every day to tend to his plants. First, you have to plant seeds, water them, care for them, remove the weeds, and then you have to pick all the plants in 70 acres! Peepaw has tractors to get the work done more efficiently so it wasn't as crazy as it sounds. In June, my Peepaw got in his tractor and headed to his field like any regular day, but he was by himself and he got hurt from falling off the tractor while moving and had to go to the hospital.

Peepaw had to stay at the hospital for two months. He could barely even pull a blanket onto him. I was shocked and sad. Almost every day, I had to go visit him for 3-6 hours. I liked visiting but not that many times! I could be with my friends or doing something I wanted to do, but instead, I was stuck with my family in the hospital. All I would do is exchange a hello with Peepaw and sit on the bench (probably drinking juice because they had unlimited free drinks at the hospital hehe). Sometimes other family members would be at the hospital such as my grandma who would be there, so I could talk with her. After a couple of days, I got bored just sitting on the bench and started a conversation with Peepaw. Eventually, I began to talk with him every time I came. We got to know each other a lot better and I actually enjoyed coming to visit.

My father would spend the night at the hospital many times to keep my great grandpa company. He only got about one hour of sleep a night, because there were always nurses and doctors coming in. My grandma (my great grandpa's daughter) and my aunt (also my great grandpa's daughter) were the ones that worked the most. They were at the hospital every single day talking to the nurses, asking questions, bringing my grandpa gifts, trying to find a home helper, spending the night, and so much more. Although they were tired, they still put my great grandpa first.

I think it was the hardest for my Peepaw. The day he got hurt, it occurred unexpectedly. Without packing or preparing anything he had to spend time away from home for two months! It's depressing to be in the hospital for so long, but what I admire is how he stayed positive through it all, still being able to make me laugh. My great grandpa made the best of the situation although he was uncomfortable all the time. What helped Peepaw was that the people he cared about were supporting him through the entire journey.

Change is hard. Believe me I know. But I also know it might seem bad at first but it also might turn into a blessing. Yes, my great grandpa got hurt, but our family got closer in the process. My great grandpa is now 99, in a wheelchair, and needs more help than he did before. Through it all, he still has the best attitude out there. I now appreciate and want to help my family more, due to that experience. I am also more grateful for my family in general, especially Peepaw. I now realize how hard they work for me and everyone else. My great grandpa is not just called great because he is old, he is called great because he is the greatest grandpa ever.

Ambedo

By Queenie Quan (Finalist)

It was a strange thing. Some would consider it to be quite peculiar if they could only see it as well, but as far as she knew, only she has been able to see the flower petals. It plagued her like a disease. Never really understanding why flower petals would cascade off her or why with every cough she would find another petal in the palm of her hand.

She would always let them fall, silently and unseen to all.

--

His piercing silver eyes held an intense familiarity, an unknown sense of longing that was never understood. Curiously he watched as the soft-spoken girl who sat two seats diagonally in front of him release a single translucent flower petal from her right hand and let it flutter ever so lightly to the classroom floor. Without so much a sound, it landed curved upward as the ultraviolet light from the classroom reflected off of the petal

173

shining glittering colors onto any object near it.

He doesn't remember when exactly he began to notice these light shining flower petals, but it had been like this for the past few months since the school year has started. For some reason, however, he seems to be the only one that has taken notice of this curiosity. It has always been simply routine, only a small handful of petals would be surrounding her desk. For some reason though, today was different.

With a shift in her seat, more translucent, yet iridescent, petals fell to the ground. This time there was enough to cover the floor around her feet, almost reaching up to her ankles. The soft petals overlapped one another, seeming to gently brush against her shoes as she adjusted her footing ever so slightly on the floor.

His eyes shifted across the room in wonderment if any other of their classmates noticed this oddity, but just as he expected, not one spared even a small glance to what only he saw.

It was after the school day had ended that he finally began to come to terms with this unique vision he had. Interestingly enough, it was the sudden blooming iridescent flowers that led him to her.

They began slowly but stayed consistent. As more bloomed in every location he glanced over, it began to burn one singular question into his mind: "Why me?"

As he moved in the direction of where the flowers grew the most abundant, he was lead down a path to the bridge that oversaw a vast emerald blue lake. It glittered and shown in the afternoon sunlight reflecting even more light to his direction as the blooms swayed in the wind. Here was where he was not expecting to see her.

--

After the day had ended she somehow found herself sitting upon the railing that overlooked the glistening lake. One leg swinging to and fro as the other propped up as she held on with one hand using a delicate yet tight grip as if it was the only thing that was grounding her at that moment. In the other hand, she fiddled with the one thing that has always piqued her curiosity: a translucent petal.

To an average passerby, there was nothing more to her than a typical school girl enjoying the serene afternoon day. The petal in her hand would not be seen and any other petals that cascaded off her would go unnoticed, even as the wind blew them scattered across the roads and walkways.

On that day, the bridge did not receive many visitors, just the peculiar girl and the boy with a remarkable vision.

She hadn't expected anyone to take notice of her, that was just how it always has been. But with a few steady footsteps, the boy had approached her placing himself just slightly further than arm's distance away. He turned towards the lake, placing his arms against the railing watching as the sky began to slowly transition into warmer colors as the sunset.

"Isn't it pretty?"

It was hard to pinpoint exactly what she meant but just by looking out across the scenery, anything could've been accounted for as pretty. But as the light little petals danced the in the wind as they moved like butterflies reflecting prismatic colors across the water, it was simply understood that they both saw those same brilliant sights. The sunset glow illuminated the sky casting a beautiful overcast above the undisturbed nature just across the water. His visual senses were overwhelmed as he was fixated in awe of the world in front of him.

The silence that settled between them both was unknown, but not unwelcomed. There was a mutual understanding that was unspoken, not needed to be heard.

He reached out to catch a singular petal that was just about to pass him by, the first time he ever came in direct contact with the peculiar little things. She watched him with more interest as he inspected the petal carefully.

Holding it up to the light, he watched as the petal's luminous colors danced before his eyes not noticing the girl's eyes trained on him.

--

It was pure chance that the two had suddenly found the other who could possibly understand this strange gift they each were granted.

He had only wanted to understand.

While she decided maybe there was no need to fall after all.

A Dance to Remember

By JaKayla Cornish (Finalist and Honorable Mention)

"Stop, stop, stop!" The chorus of the song blaring from the studio speaker comes to an abrupt halt and the dancers come to freeze in motion as though caught.

"Half of you look as though you're trying to convince me you are depressed! Your emotion weak, and so is your technique." Her arms swinging in wide gestures to accompany her dramatic tone. "I shouldn't have to be convinced that you are feeling Adele's emotion, I , as a member of the audience, should feel it what she is feeling ."

Her graceful, confident stride across the linoleum floors in her light, airy dress made it seem as though she floated across the room. Barefoot, she made her way into the center of the group of students, where she waited to gain for all of her student's attention to be focused on her.

The students were appalled that the new teacher had the audacity to come in and teach with such strict and rigorous discipline on her first week back, but slowly gave her their attention. She continued on, unfazed by the array of countenances that did not support her being there.

"Imagine you are the artist." the choreographers says closing her eyes. "Think of a time you felt such longing for someone along with pain, or sorrow. I think of what I went through to get here. I had a choice between life and death, but who want to choose between something as fragile as the past and precious as the future? It was the biggest decision of my life, I must say."

Her last words resonated in the air above the rather eager audience and sat in a circle around her, listening intently.

I was eight years old when my parents told me they were getting a divorce. I didn't fully know what that meant until a year later I was making a trail of plastic pearly white petals for my father's new wife. I never knew how to feel about her or my dad after the wedding because we didn't keep in touch except for birthdays and holidays. He moved from Texas to Arizona and the distance did more that put miles between us. Over the years, I grew undeniably close to my mother. She never remarried. Often nights, I could make out the creaking of the front door opening and shutting as she snuck out for the night to that of the unknown. It was a struggle to not look as if I'd only slept for four hours the following morning.

When I got home from school those days I'd wake her up from her cat nap on the couch, speaking softly as she always wanted me to and presented her with the two ibuprofens and glass of water when she called for them. She'd shower and rest for another hour and wake up just in time to prepare dinner for the both of us. By dinnertime, the past twelve hours had vanished from our memories; I hadn't smelt the strong lingering scent of liquor or even seen the mascara that ran down her face. We engaged in normal conversation about my day at school and she'd take me to dance practice afterwards. That was most nights.

One Saturday mid spring my mother took me along with her to one of her doctor's appointments. Immediately and almost instinctively my brain racked for any recent changes in her appearance or behavior in her. She's hadn't seemed to be in any major pain recently, maybe slightly simmer? I couldn't think of anything drastic.

I sat in the cold, plastic seat next to my mother as we waited for her name to be called. She tried to move in carefree movements and talk about things as if the doctor couldn't give us the worst news of our life, but I could sense the concern in the way she tried to be unbothered by the situation at hand. After two long hours of watching the same heart disease campaign on the small television in the corner, we were escorted into one of the exam rooms decorated with cutouts of jungle themed animals and diagrams that did nothing to ease the tensions. The doctor came in shortly after us.

"Your tests are back from your last appointment." My brows furrowed. She hadn't mentioned that this was a follow up or that she'd come to get checked out beforehand. My concern doubled 10 fold. What was wrong that she didn't feel she needed to tell me? When she grabbed my hand almost instantly, the room dropped ten degrees and I braced myself.

"As we thought, the elevated alcohol levels have caused your scans show evidence of a tumor from stage one pancreatic cancer."

Cancer? My mother has cancer? My mother has cancer? The word was foreign on my tongue and didn't become any more recognizable the more I thought about it? How could my mother have cancer?

"This isn't time to be concerned now Karen, we can start on you on treatment as soon as you're ready." I didn't know how to feel. How are you supposed to feel when your mother is presented with cancer on silver plate?

The walk back to our car was silent; nothing we could say could justify what we'd just learned. My head was whirring as she drove off but I don't remember feeling anything. I only recall that up above the clouds above were dark and heavy, but never did a drop fall from the sky..

The day after and for weeks and so on, it was as if we didn't even go to the doctor's office. I'd guess she wasn't ready to face reality. I began to wonder why she wanted me to come along with her if we only planned to not talk about it. She hadn't ask me to go along with her when she went out at night and we didn't talk about those nights. There was no change in her diet, there was no change in activity, and there was no change at all. The sky was still cloudy the conversation still normal. Things were okay, at first.

However as years passed, the cancer showed its monstrous ways. My mother, I'd noticed had loss of distinct amount of weight by the time I graduated and gained a slight yellow tint to her pallid skin. Some days she was in too much pain to go to work but was never in enough to go get help. I felt like to continually pester her about her condition would only make it worse. Eventually, we were both ignoring the elephant in the room and definitely weren't ready for when it came charging in.

An unknown number caused my phone to buzz loudly on my mother's hospital bedside table. I hadn't been expecting any calls from my friends because they knew I would be cooped up alongside my mom bedside. I failed to even try to socialize.

I let the phone ring a couple times to give the caller the option to hang up before finally answering.

"Hello?" I said tentatively.

"Hello," a deep voice resonates the receiver. "It's uh, it's Dad."

I didn't know what to say. I couldn't think of any specific reason why he would be calling today.

"I know we don't talk very much," he says to fill the silence I created, "but I have some important information that you might want to know." I don't say anything.

"I ran into an old friend and he just so happened to have started work at Martin's Performing Arts School here in Arizona, you know, the one you've been talking about? I told him about you and he says that they would love to have you teach their new dance academy."

"I, I-" I stutter out,

"You don't have to answer to me, I'll give you the information and you can decide on your own time." He says. I receive an email almost immediately after.

I can't count how many times I read and reread the email my father forwarded to me from the art school.

"You should choose the school, you know." My mother says groggily as she fixes her scarf. A blond strand falls to her shoulder.

"I don't think I will." But I can't look at her in her eyes.

"Honey, you being here will neither speed up nor slow down this disease. It's coming for me sweetie- it's here actually," she chuckles and coughs. "I know you think you should stay, for me- but I don't want to be the reason why you pass up your dream job. I don't and wouldn't want anything or anyone, rather, to deter you from your dreams."

Clicking on 'Compose' I began to write my response to Martin's Performing Arts Academy.

"Thanks for all your help!" I exclaim as I push the last box of CD's into a corner. I walk my coworker out of my studio and inhale the fresh new paint that coated the walls. From the hairs on my head to the toes on my feet, I was ecstatic. My heart beated in excitement for the new semester. I couldn't wait for the paint scent to be replaced with perspiration, rosin, and a the familiar clashing of perfumes, colognes, and deodorants. Breathing out, I opening my eyes from my delightful dream of my soon reality, and my phone rings.

"Hello?" I answer.

"Hello, this is Nurse Heather from Houston's Methodist Hospital, is this Karen McArthur's daughter?

"Yes," I stammer.

"Your mother suffered a complication during surgery. You should come to the hospital as soon as possible."

My mother's funeral was short and brief, the way she would have wanted it, however my grief was quite the opposite. As I lay in bed in my mother's home, I felt as if the once eager girl who'd finally come to peace with her life had been snatched away from my body and left with a void that nothing could fill. How could I even try to teach a class full students with a heart so heavy and dark?

I sent a letter to the school expressing my most sincere apologies, and hoped they would find a suitable substitute in my absence. I hadn't planned on going back, in fact I hadn't bothered to stretch or dance even if things got better. Most days, I solemnly listened to whatever played when I hit shuffle on my iPod.

A day before the fourth week of school, I sat on the couch trying to ignore the emotional pain that my physical body accepted as its own. Shuffle played song after song that I choreographed dances to, but I couldn't bring myself to perform any one. Suddenly, a melody played that I hadn't heard since I was a little girl. Even knowing that the song was initially written for two lovers, I couldn't help but think of my mom as the lyrics sang to me. The strongest of emotions began to arise at the thought of her and I couldn't fight my natural urge to get up and pour them out through dance any longer. As I swayed and twirled rhythmically to the music, the reasons why my mother told me to choose the school were revelations I'd finally come to truly understand. It was only because she loved me to let me go and become who I wanted to be, to not hold me captive to her bedside and have us both watch each other deteriorate. Nothing done now or then would bring her back, so why must I wallow in her dwelling as if that will too?

As soon as the last note resonated, I packed my bags back up to Arizona I drove with "Do You Remember" thumping from my speakers.

Back at the studio in Arizona I decided to observe as a visitor before I introduced myself to my class. The students were stretching and I smiled warmly as nostalgia rushed through my veins. I missed it. The smell of sweaty feet and perfume charged through me with the foreign feeling of true contentment. I knew this was where I wanted to be. This was where I belonged.

The choreographer stood up from her warm spot center of attention and brushed the imaginary dust from her flowy dress and surveyed her student's faces. They all mocked awe and appreciation from her story, but in them she could see that they could feel what she felt.

"Do you feel that?" she asks her class. They nod.

"That's how your audience should feel when you dance."

Cool Imagination Titles

Convergence by Brian Claspell
    Jim Conrad may not be as fictional as the CIA thinks. Pick up *Convergence*, a mystery-thriller, on Amazon and at other fine retailers.

One Spark *- Short Story Anthology 2011-2018*
    Enjoy reading the short stories of all the winners (2011-2018) and 2018 finalist of the "Imagination Begins with You…" high school writing contest. All proceeds support scholarships.

One Spark *– "Imagination Begins with You…" 2019*
    Jump into reading finalist stories from the "Imagination Begins with You…" high school writing contest. All proceeds support scholarships.

www.ingramcontent.com/pod-product-compliance
Lightning Source LLC
Chambersburg PA
CBHW030328180626
46810CB00003B/1273